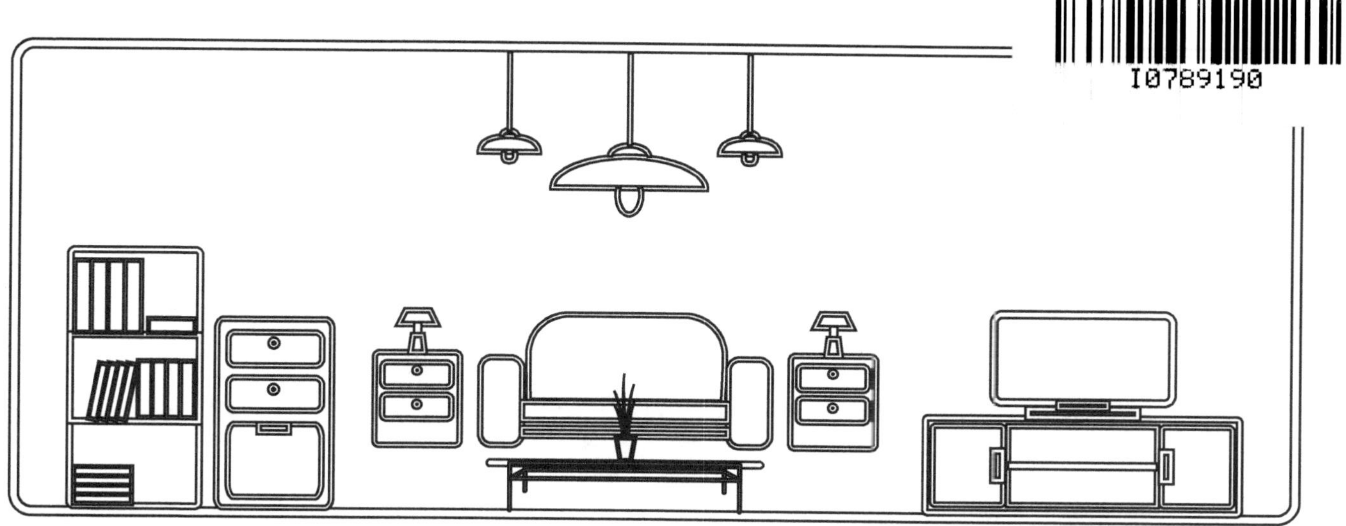

THIS BOOK BELONGS TO :

____

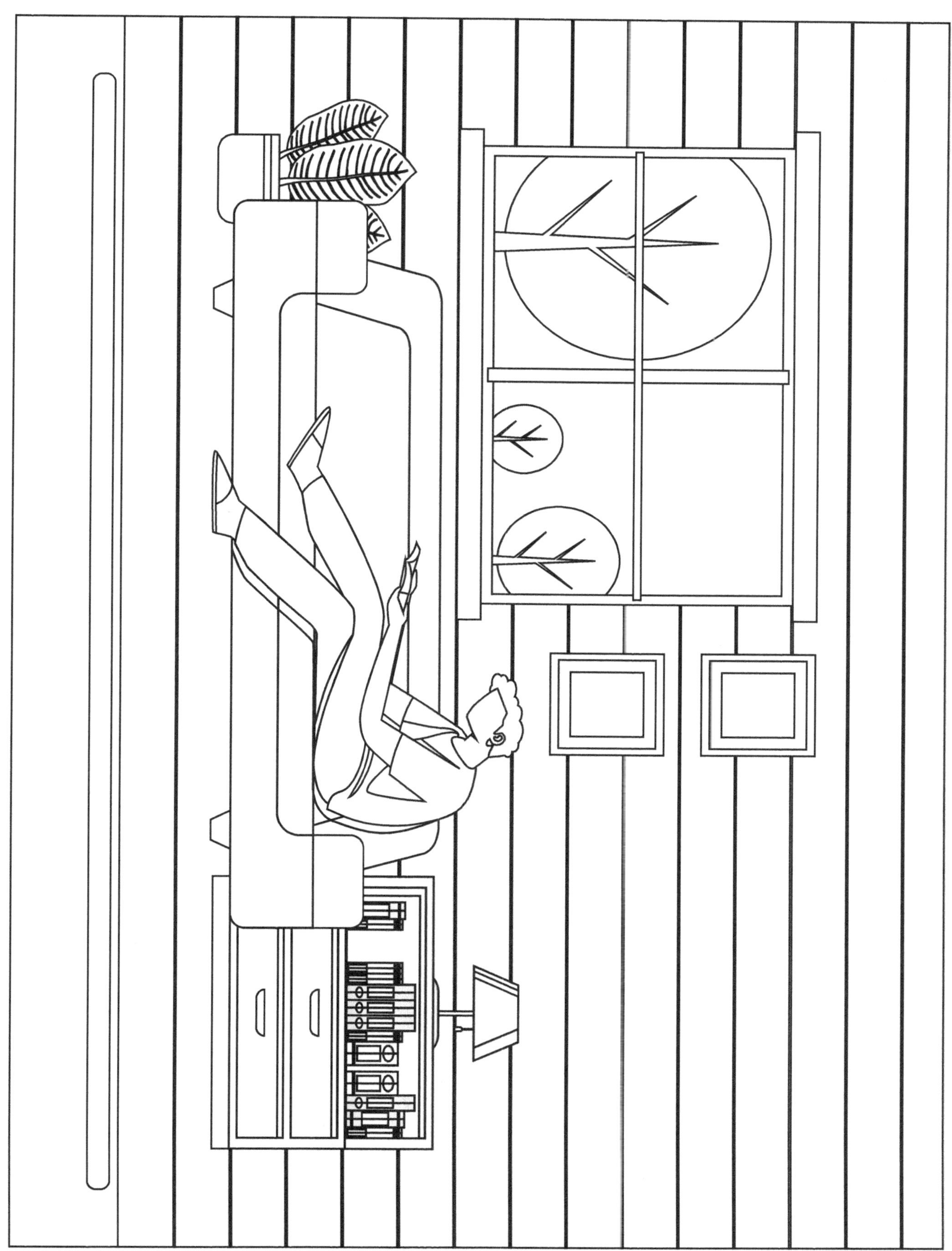

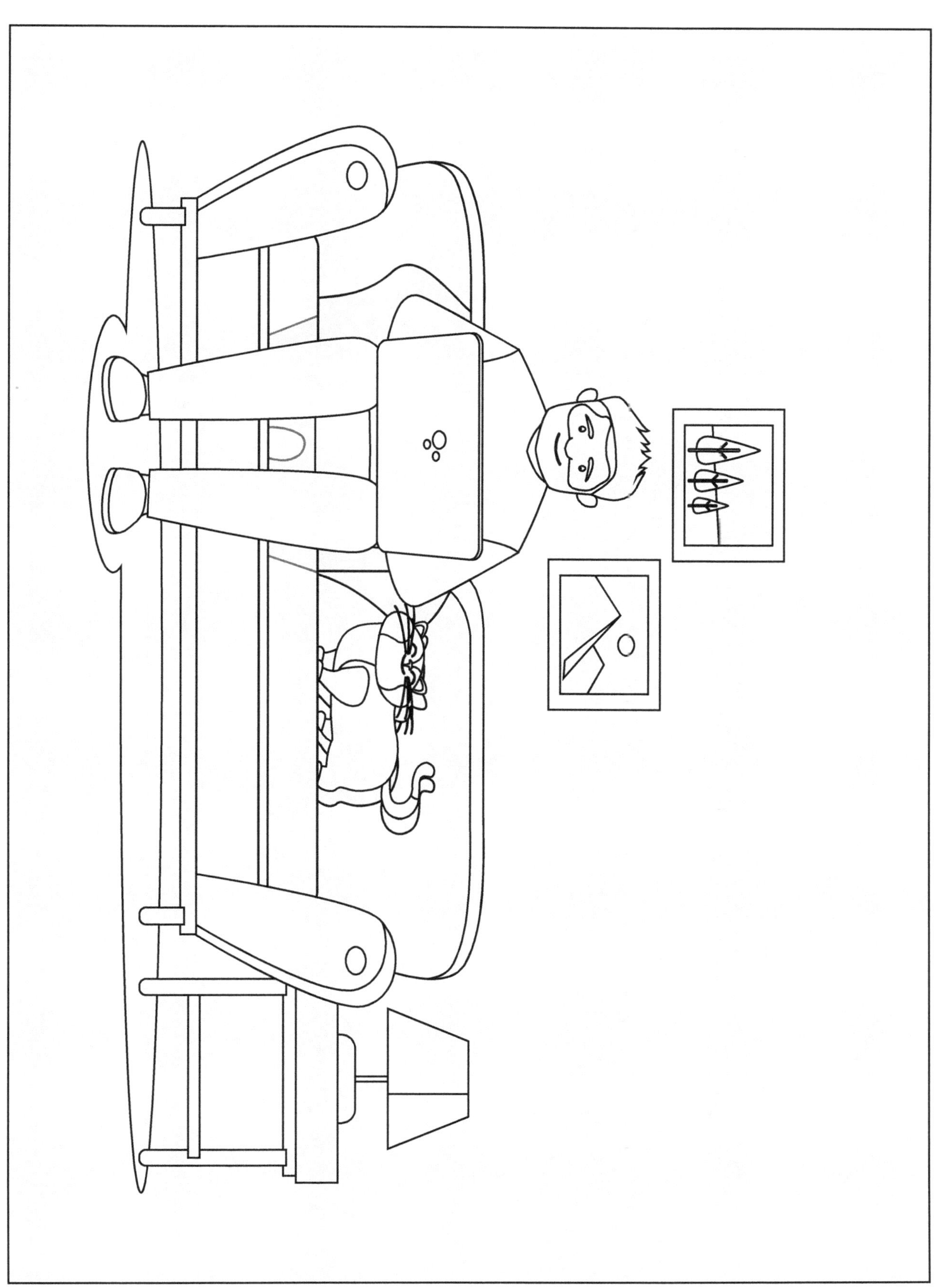

HOME
sweet
HOME

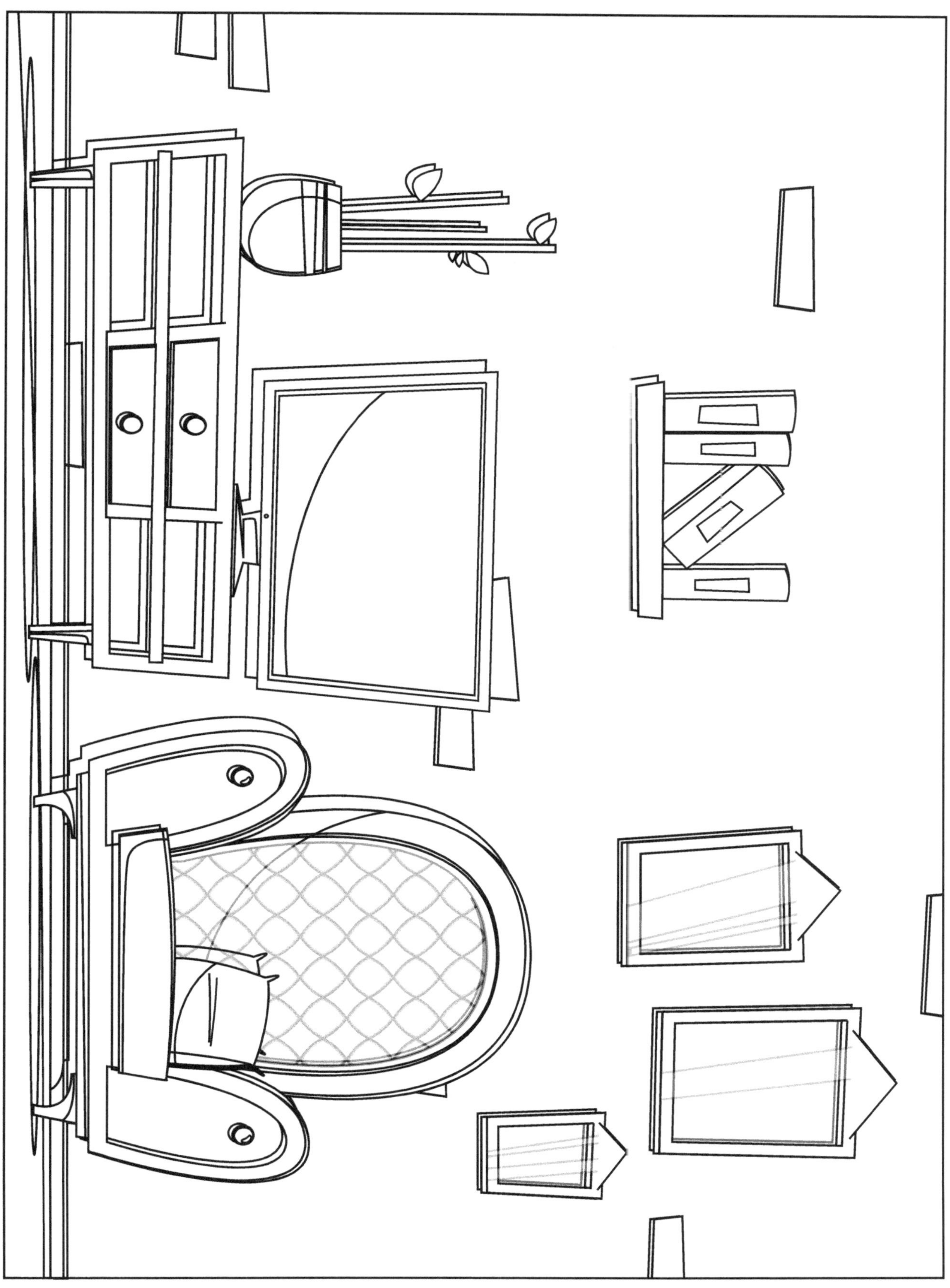

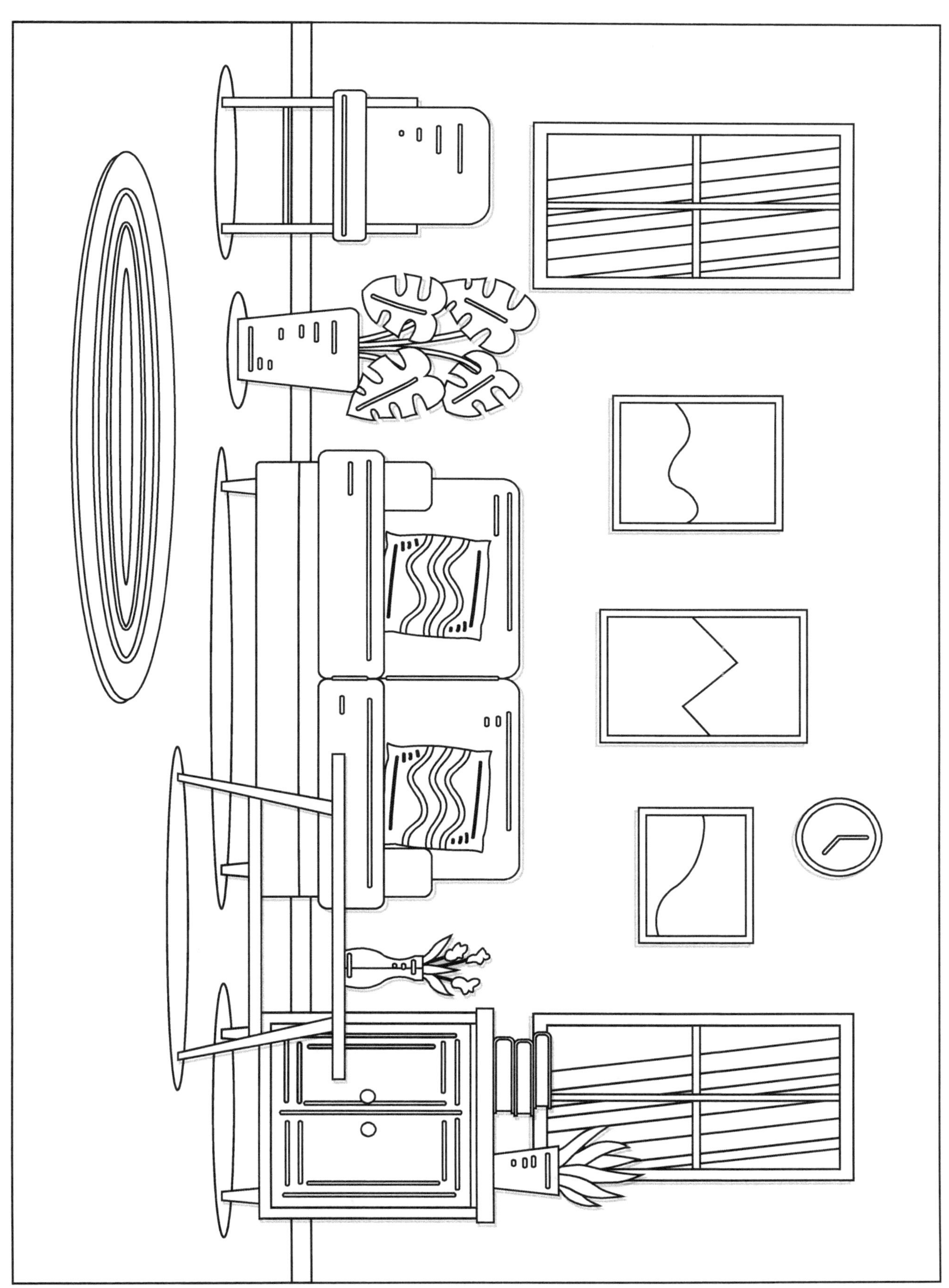

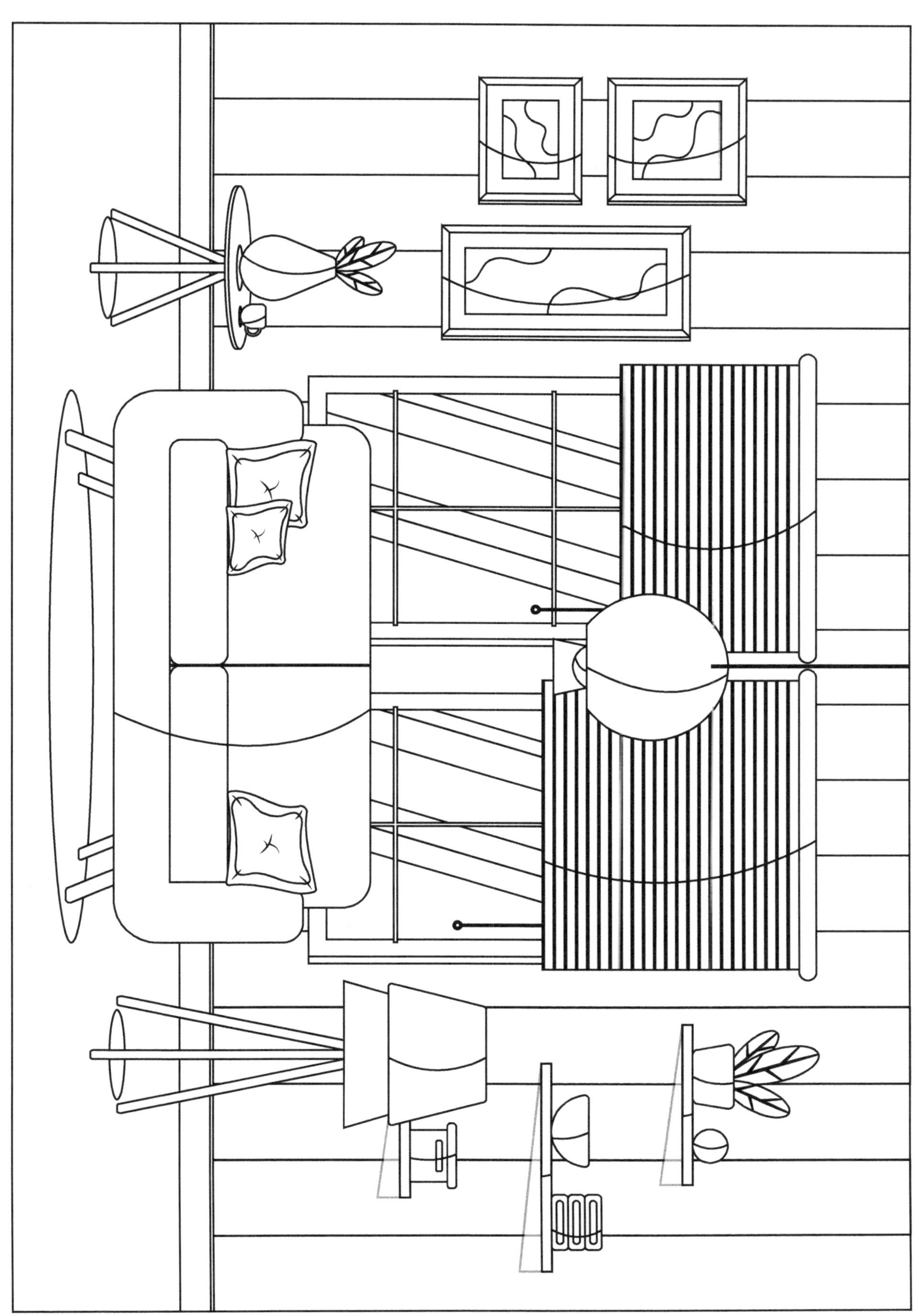

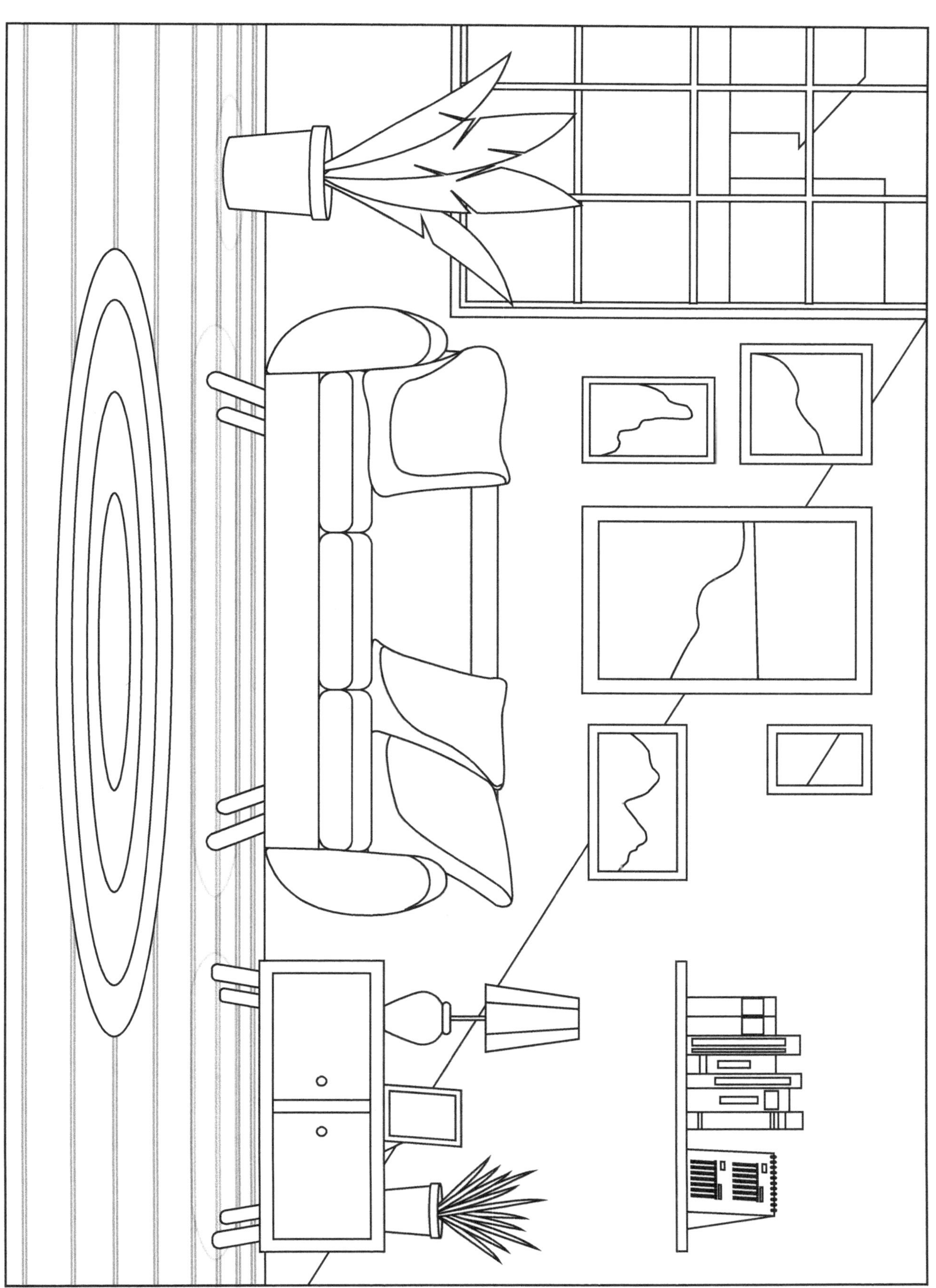

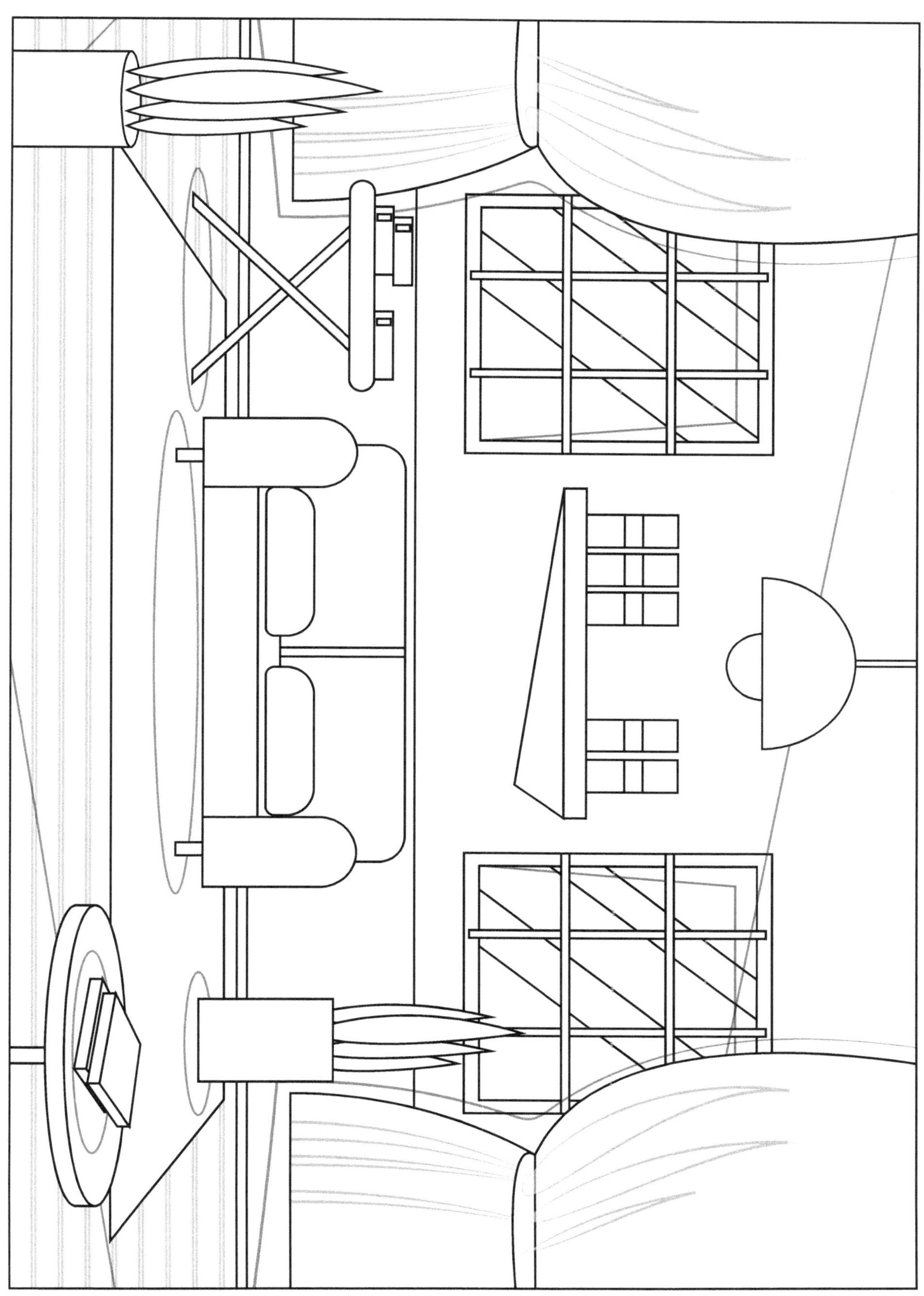

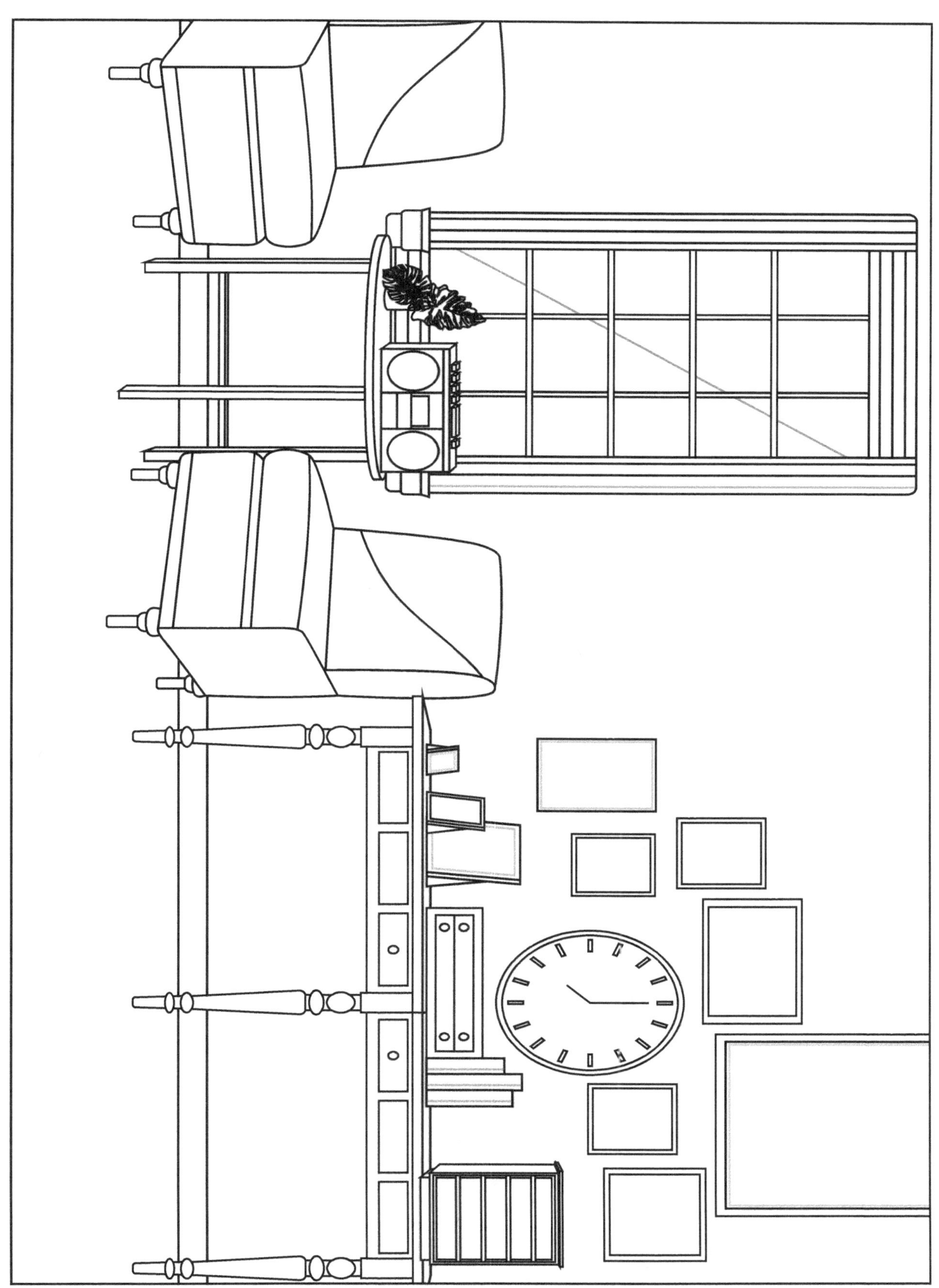

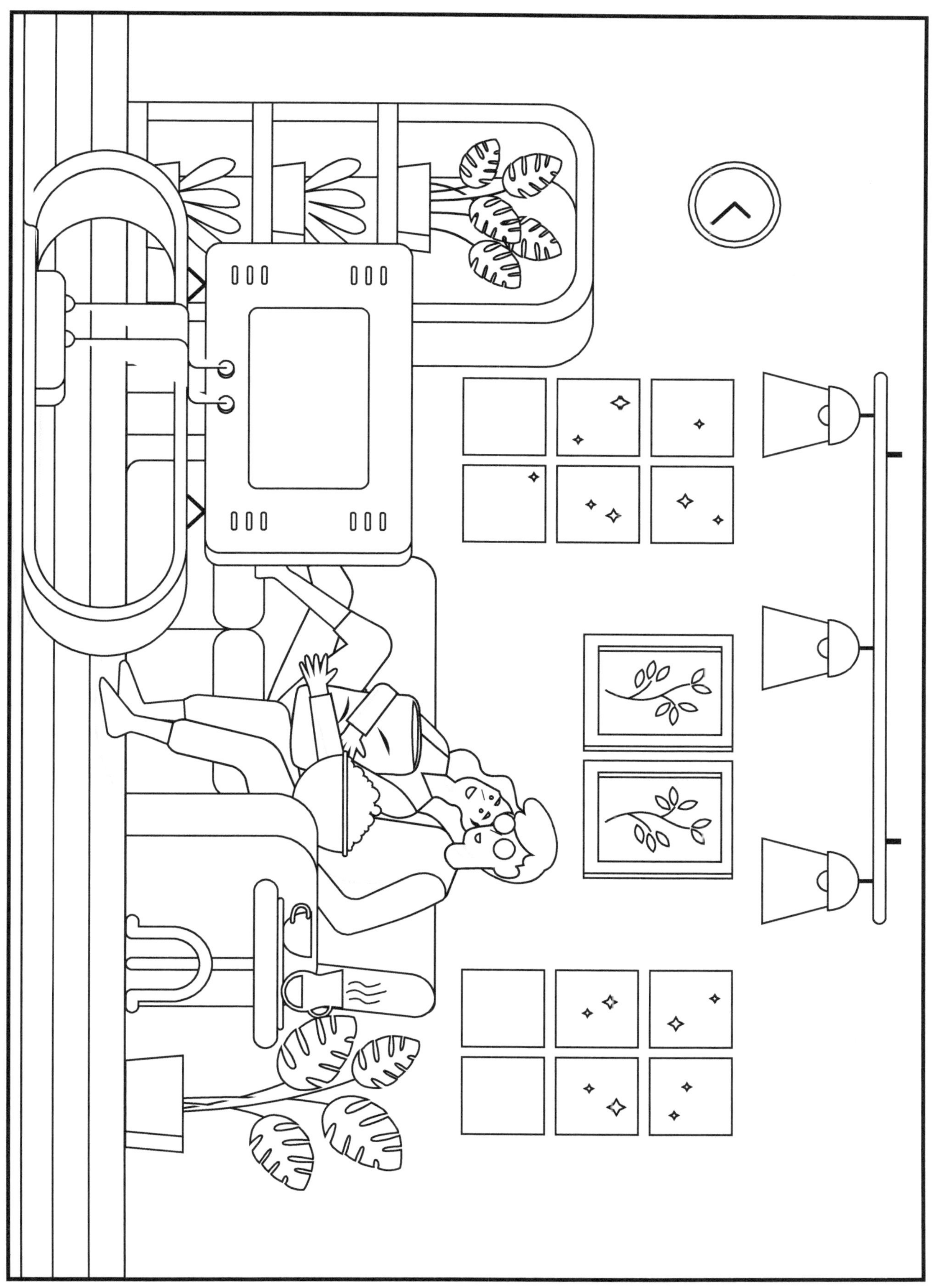

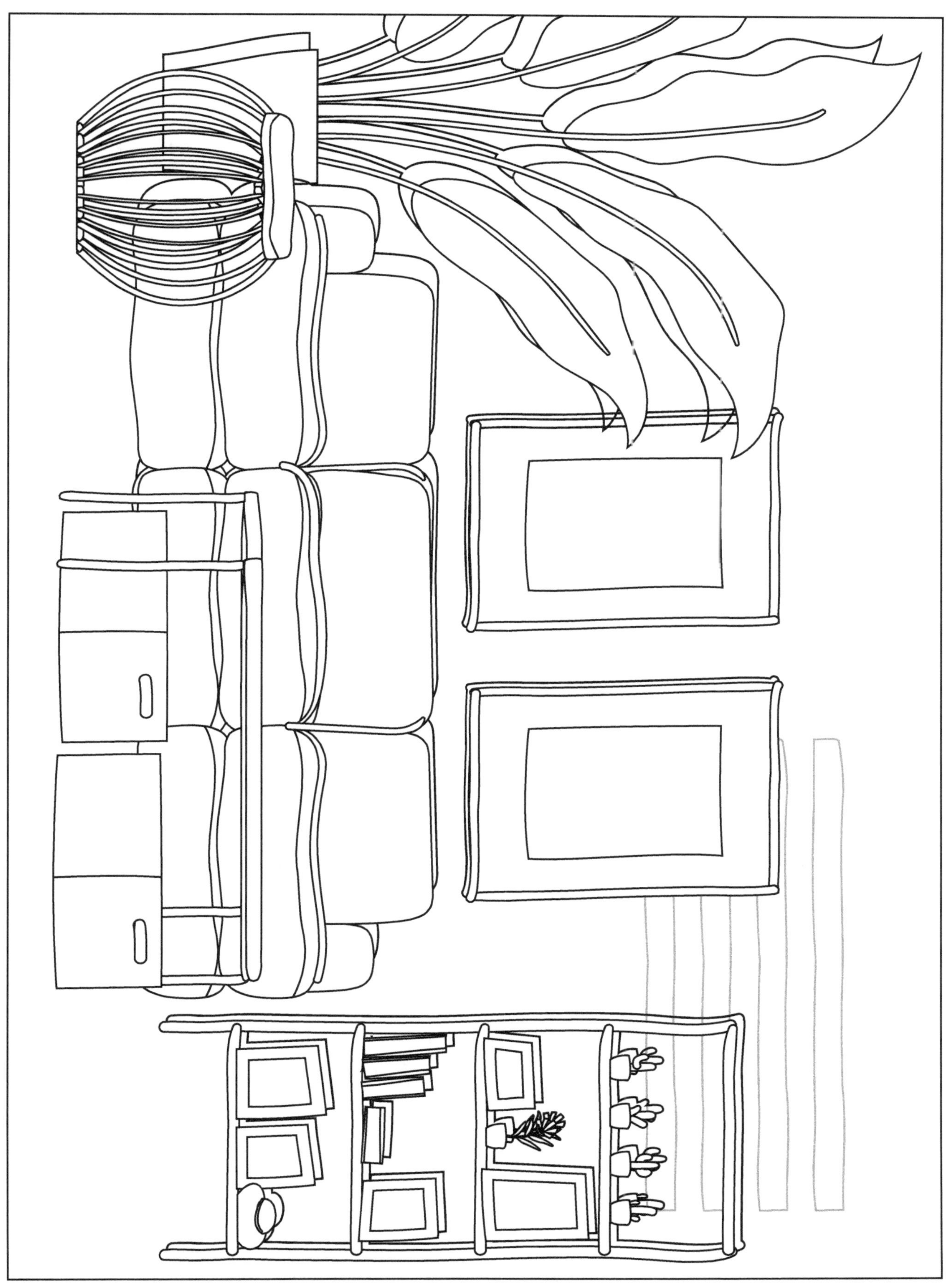

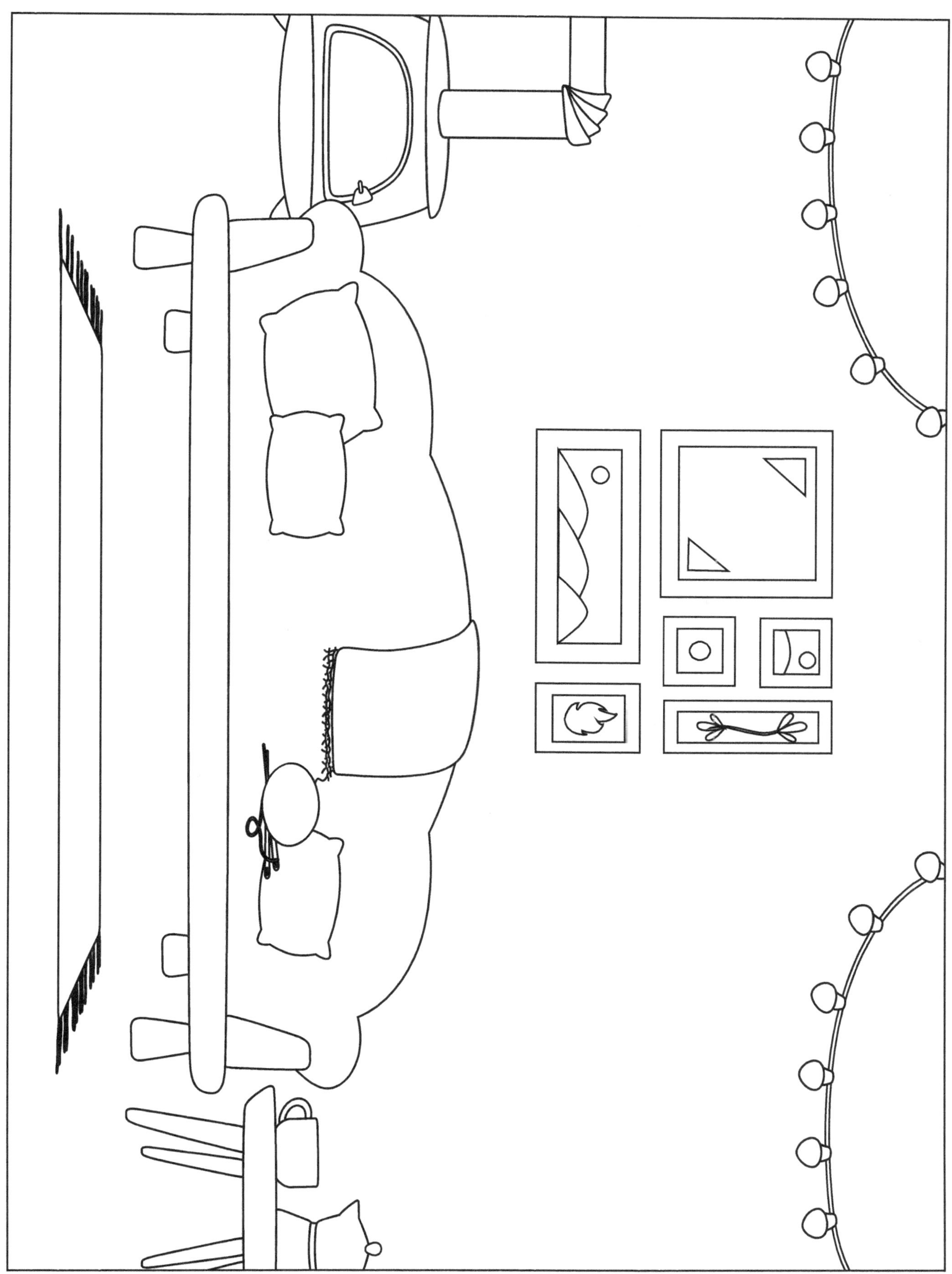

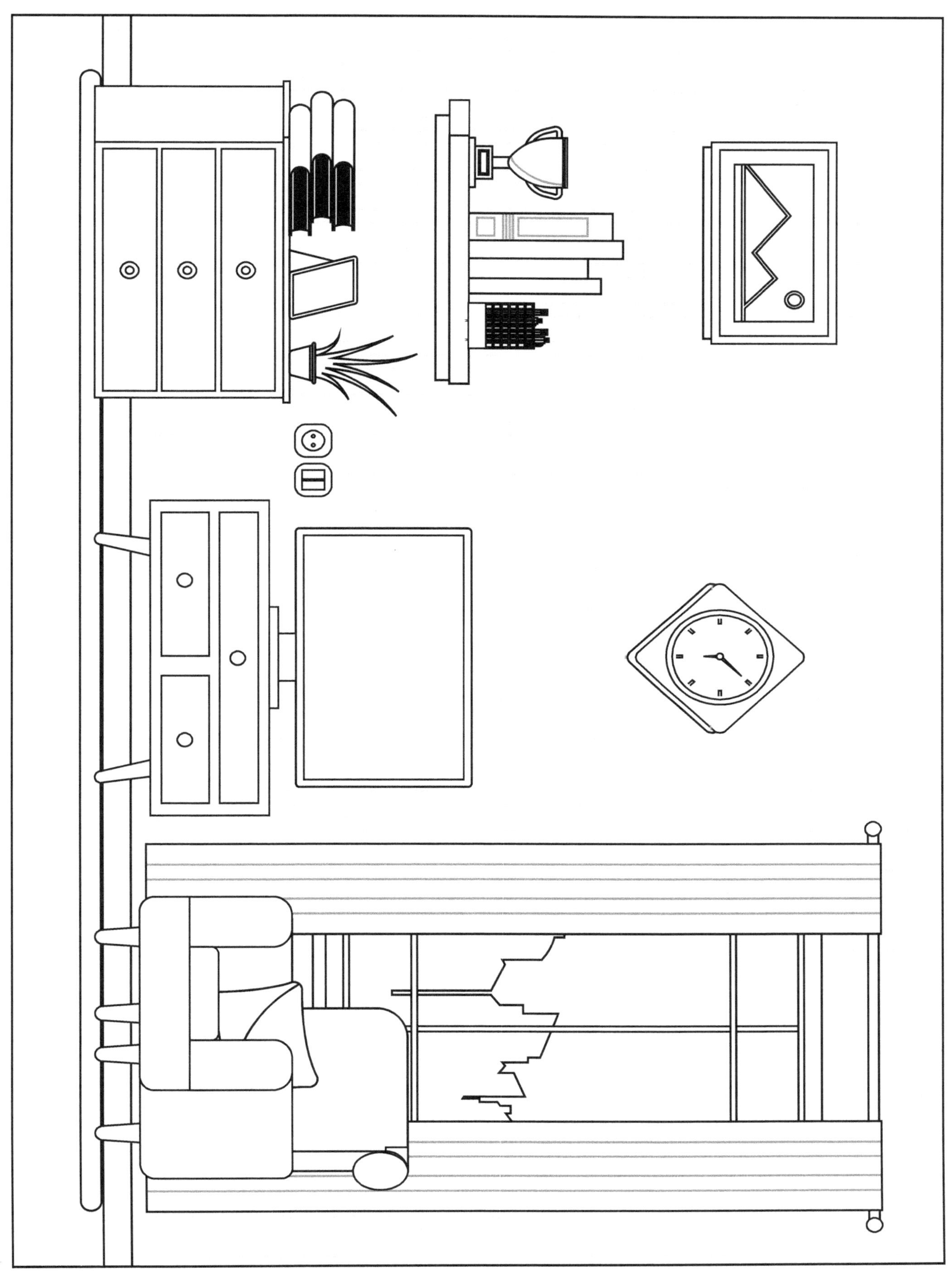

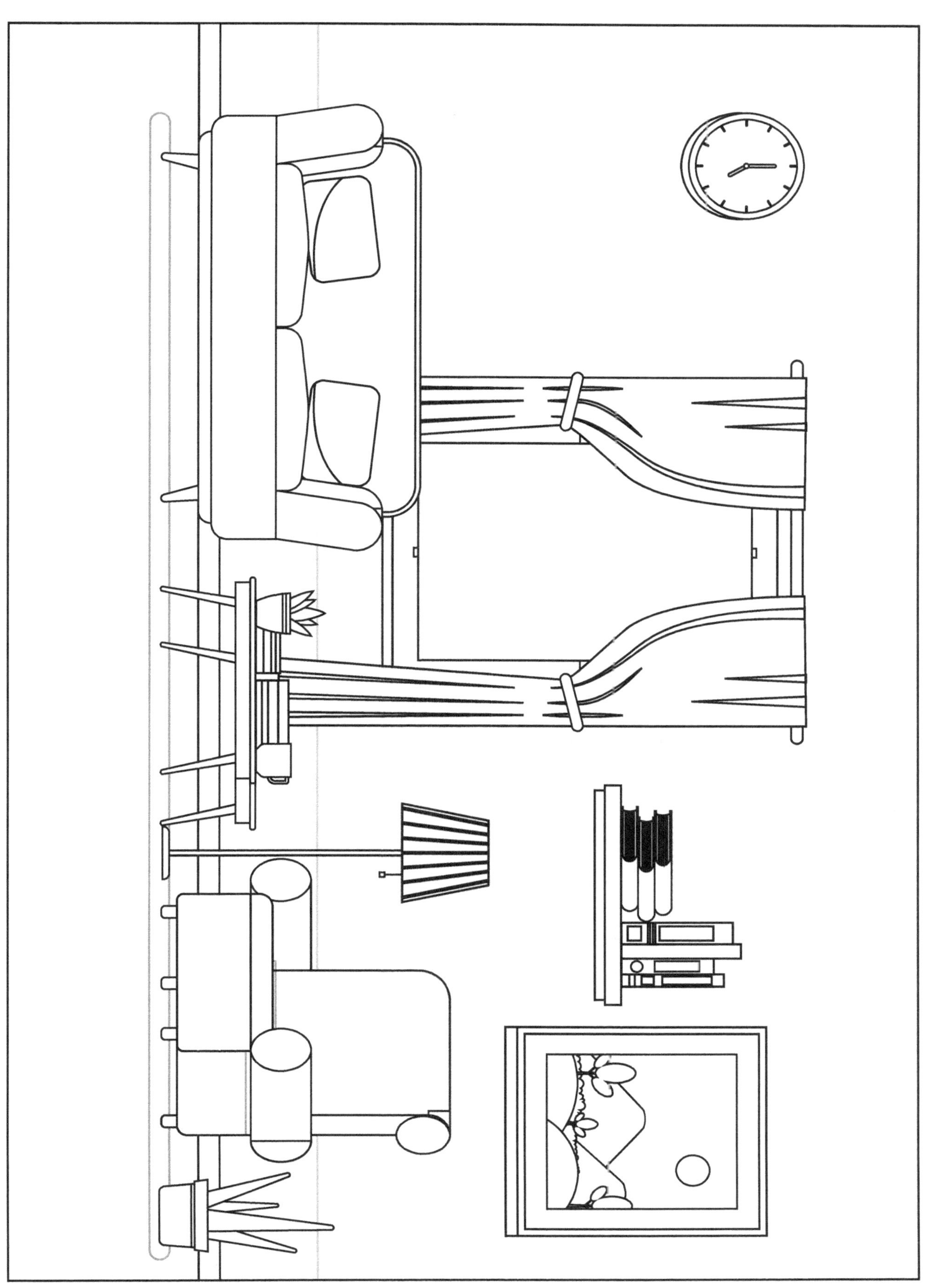

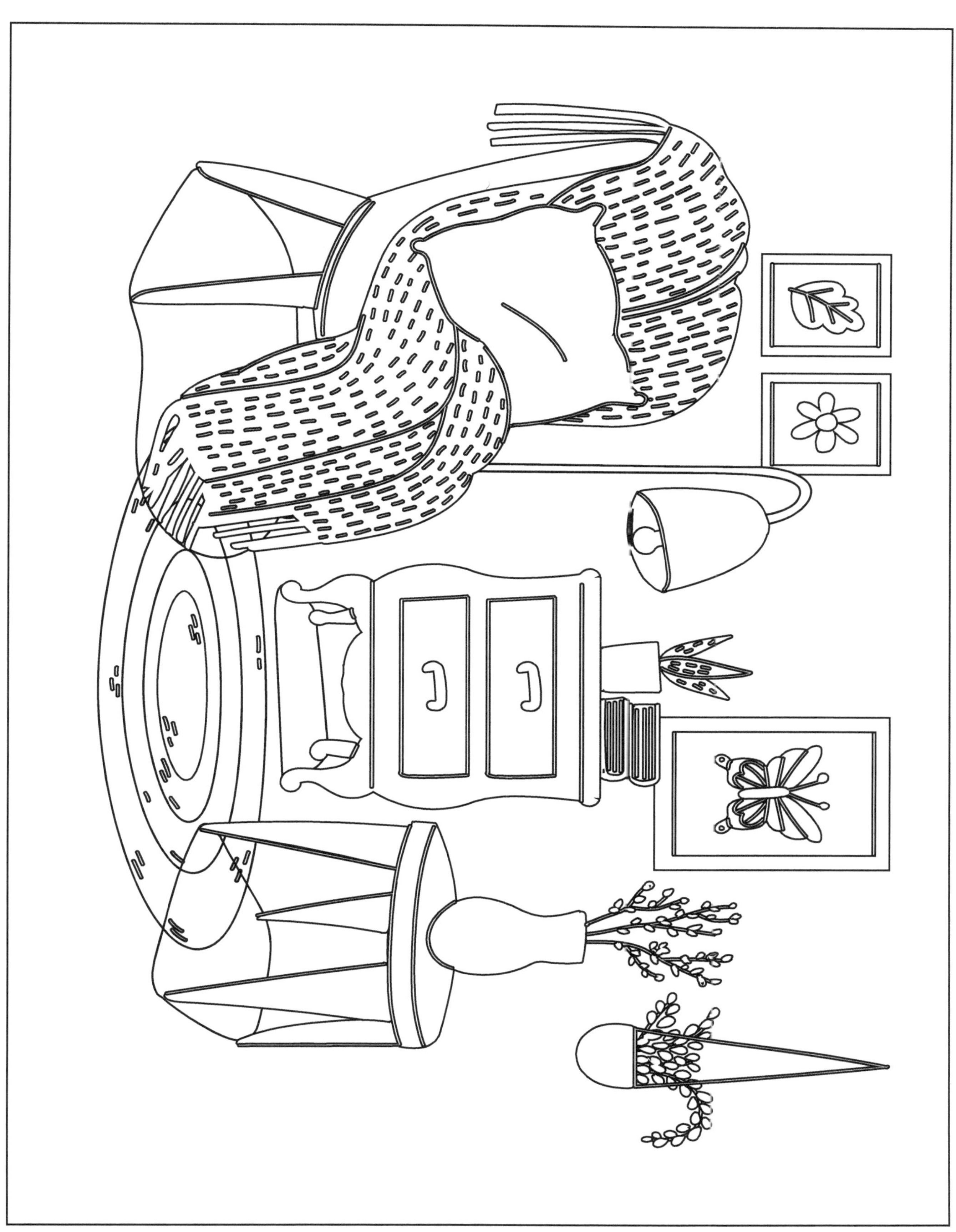

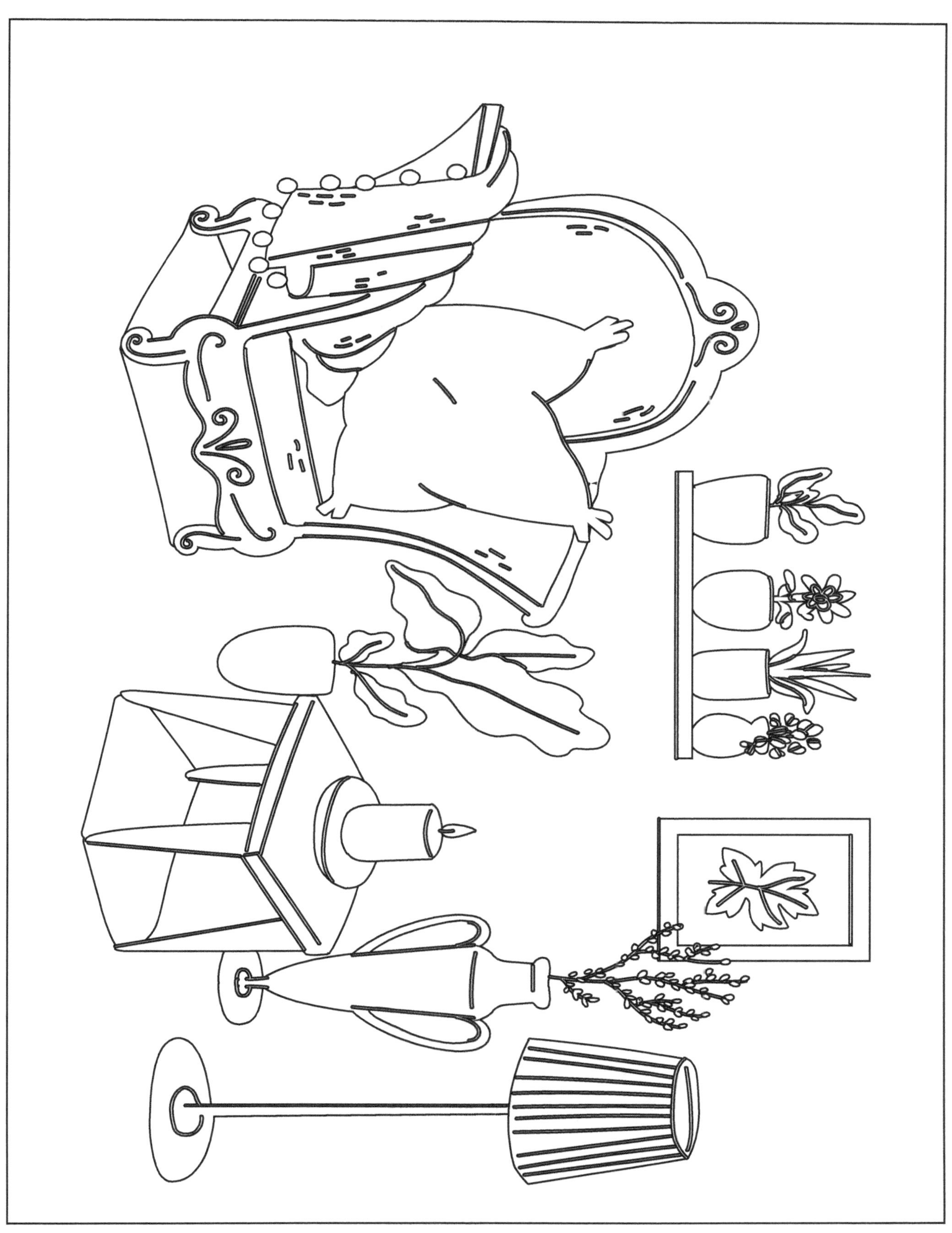

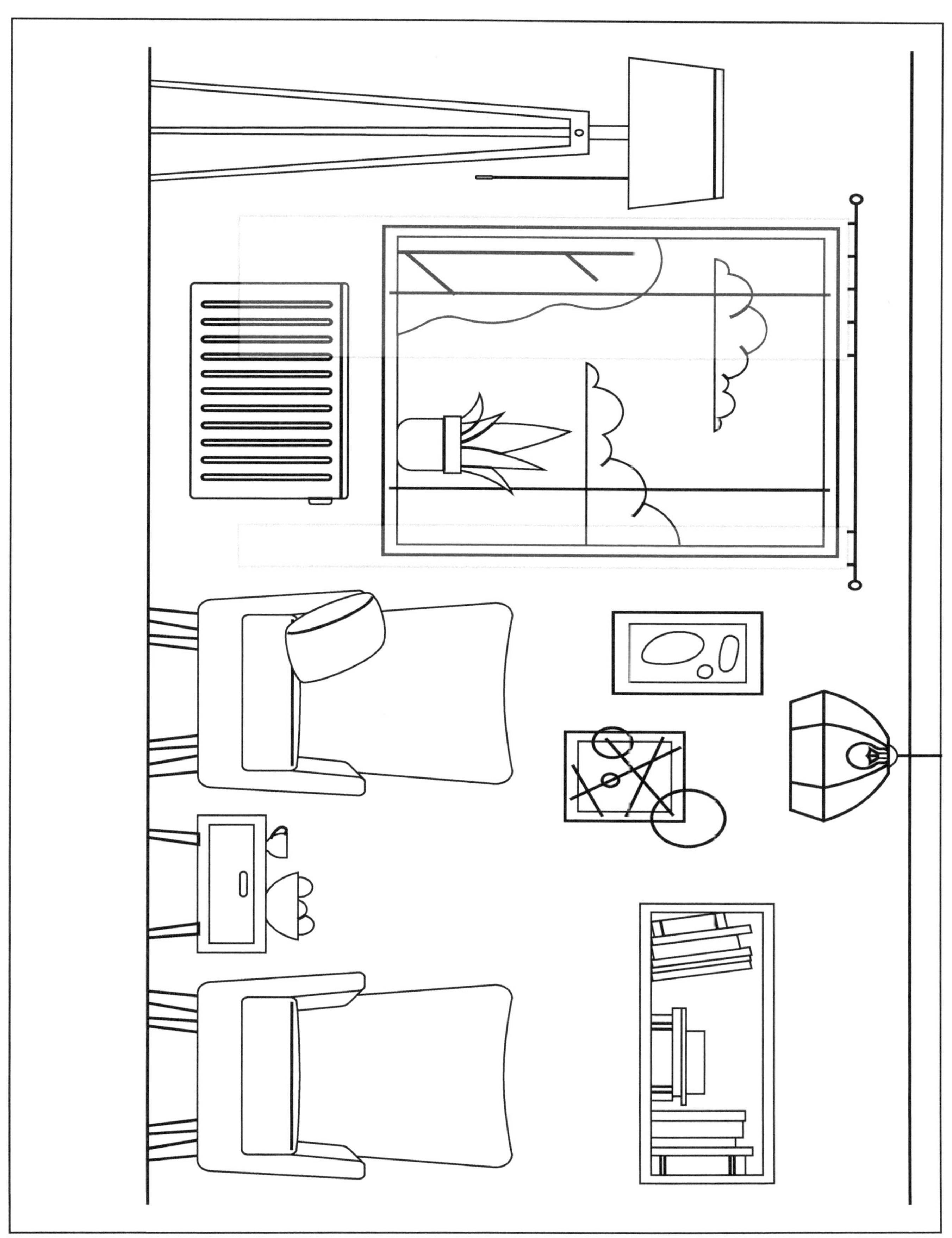

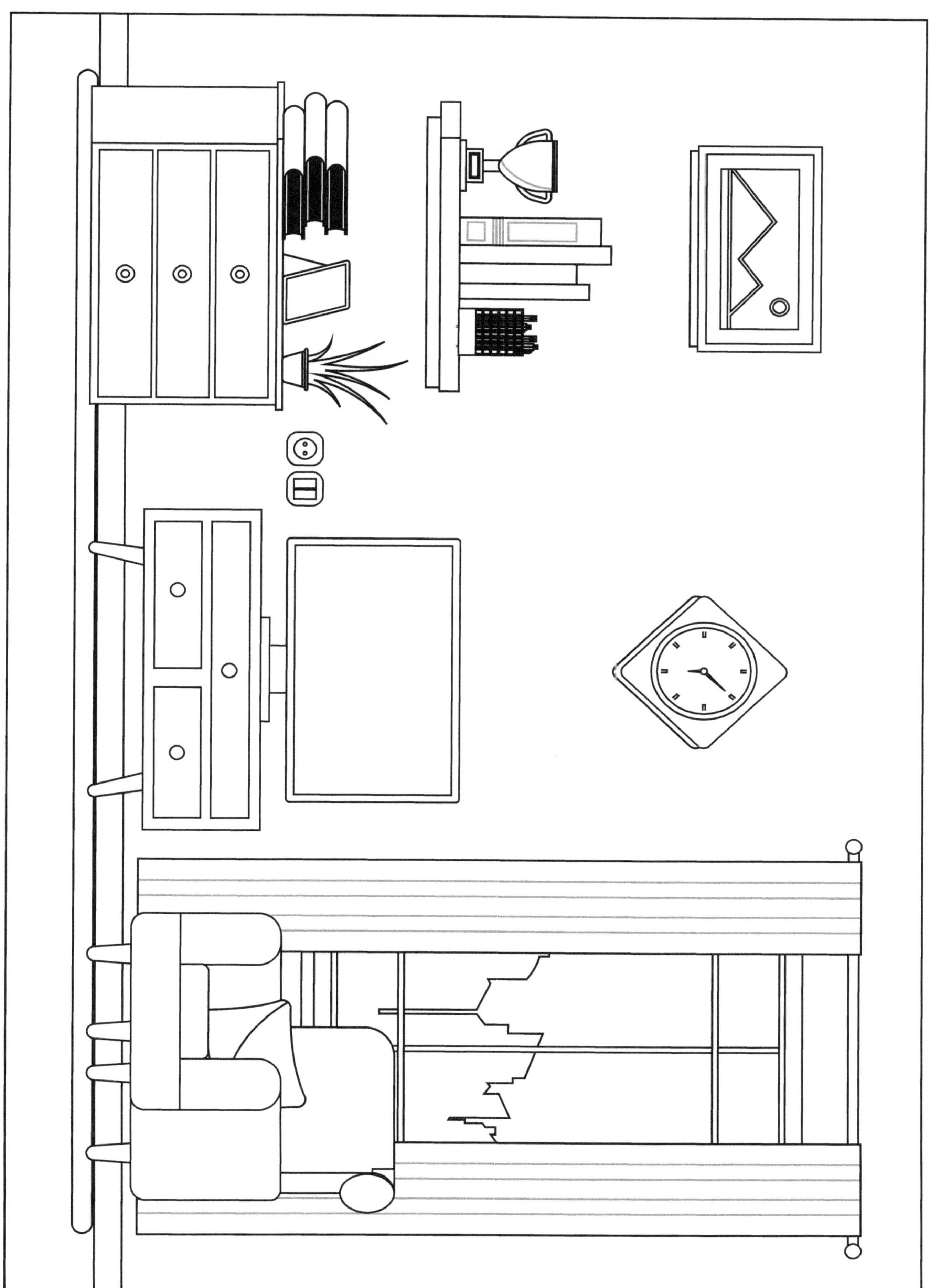

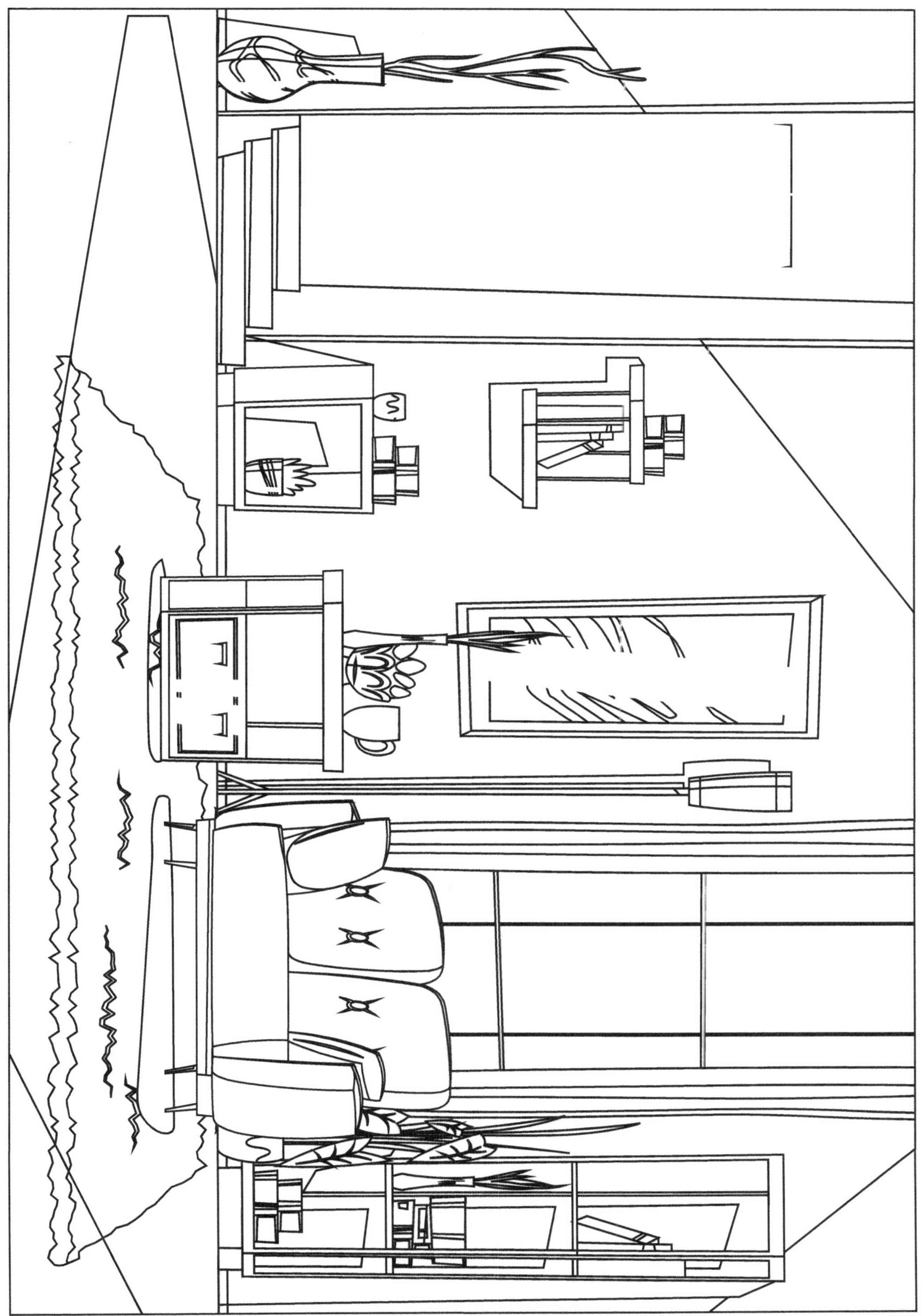

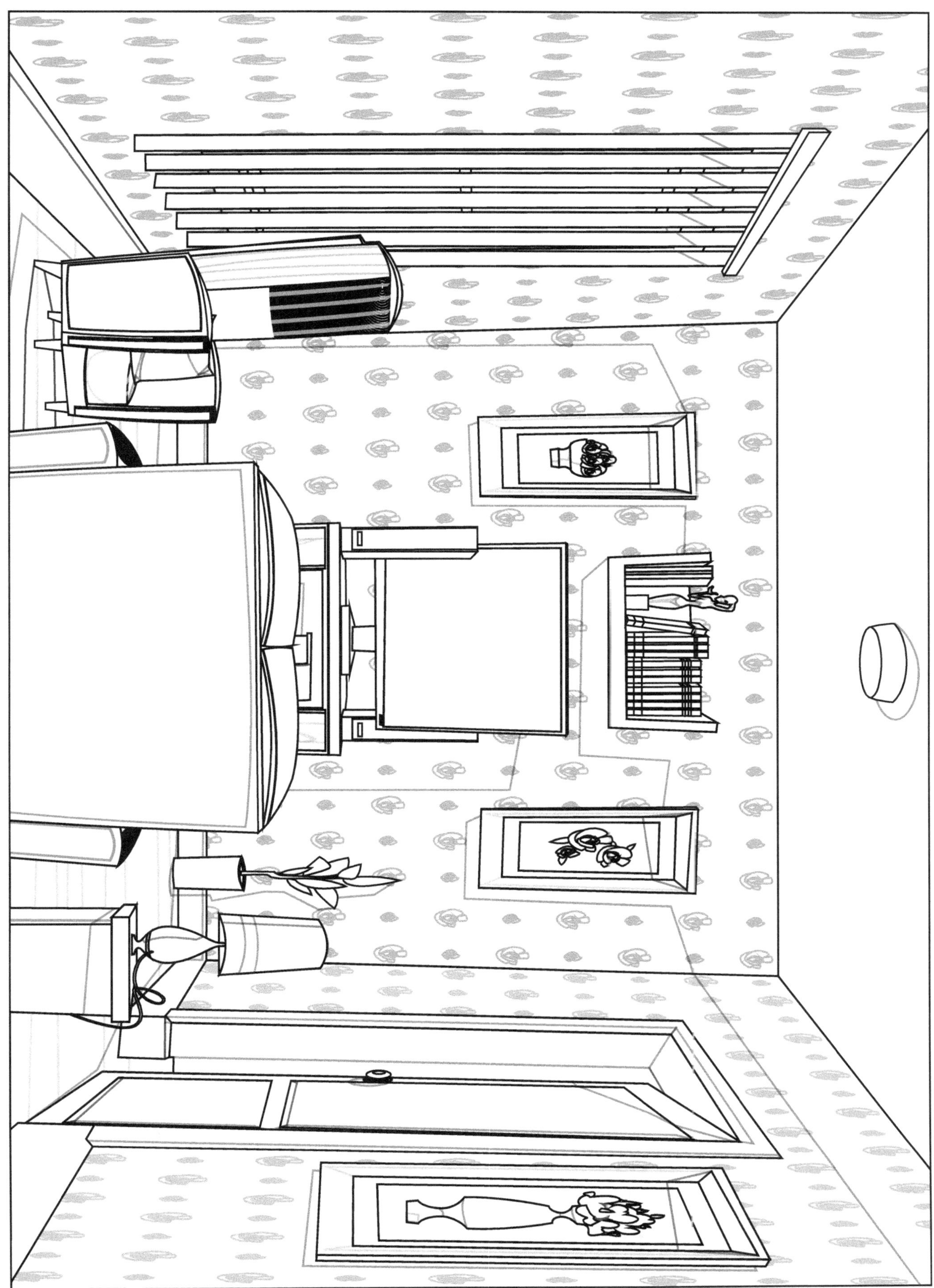

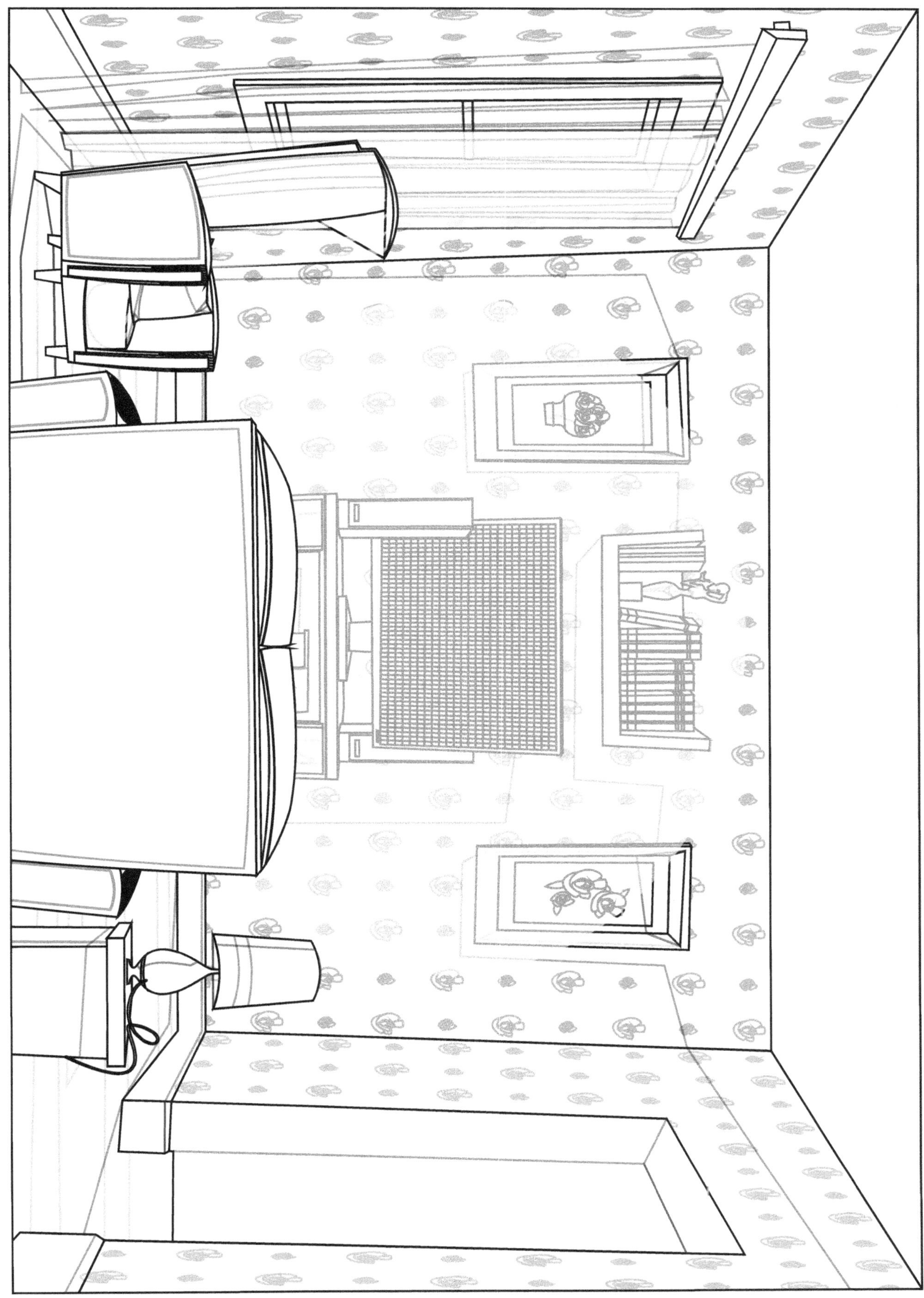

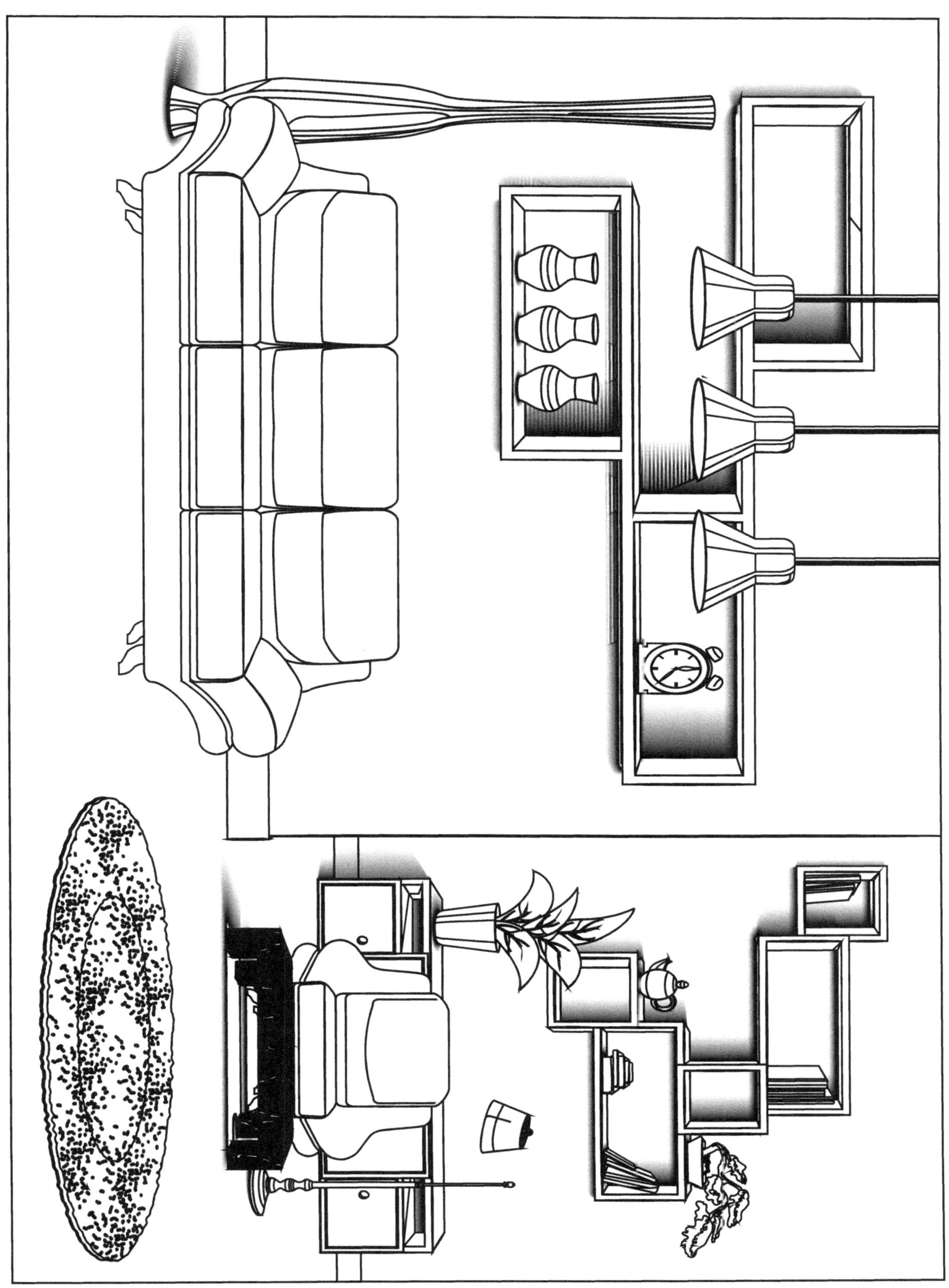

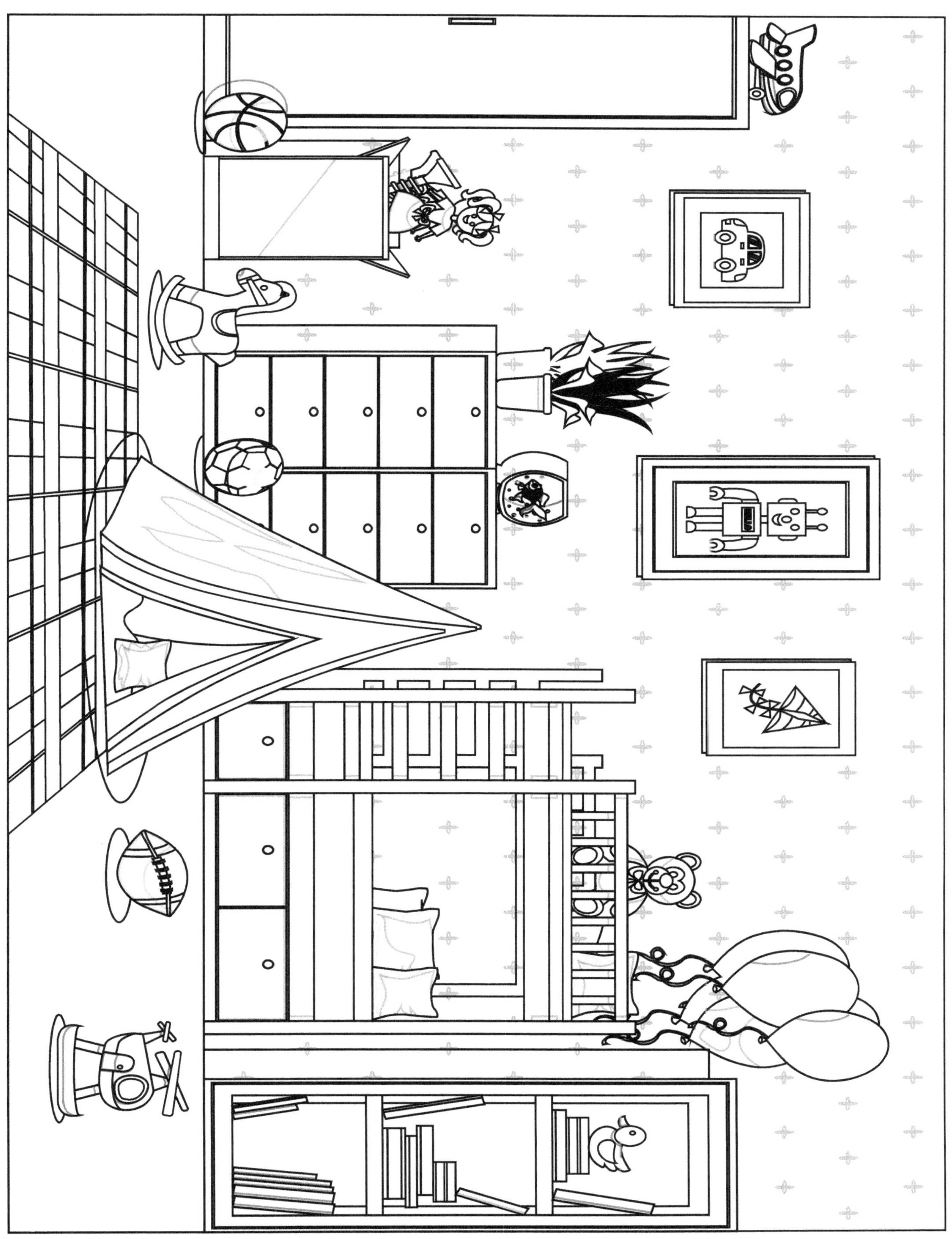

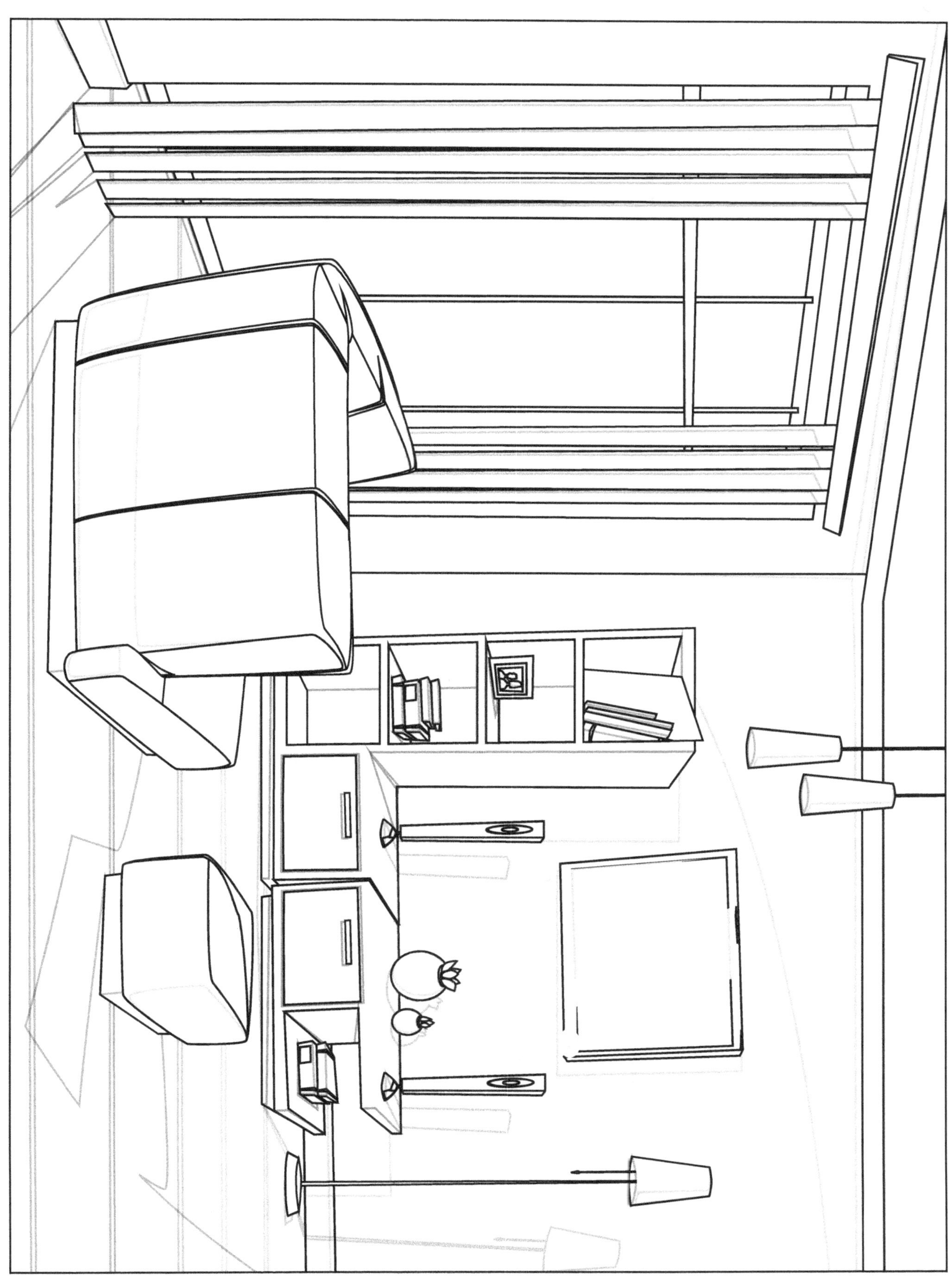

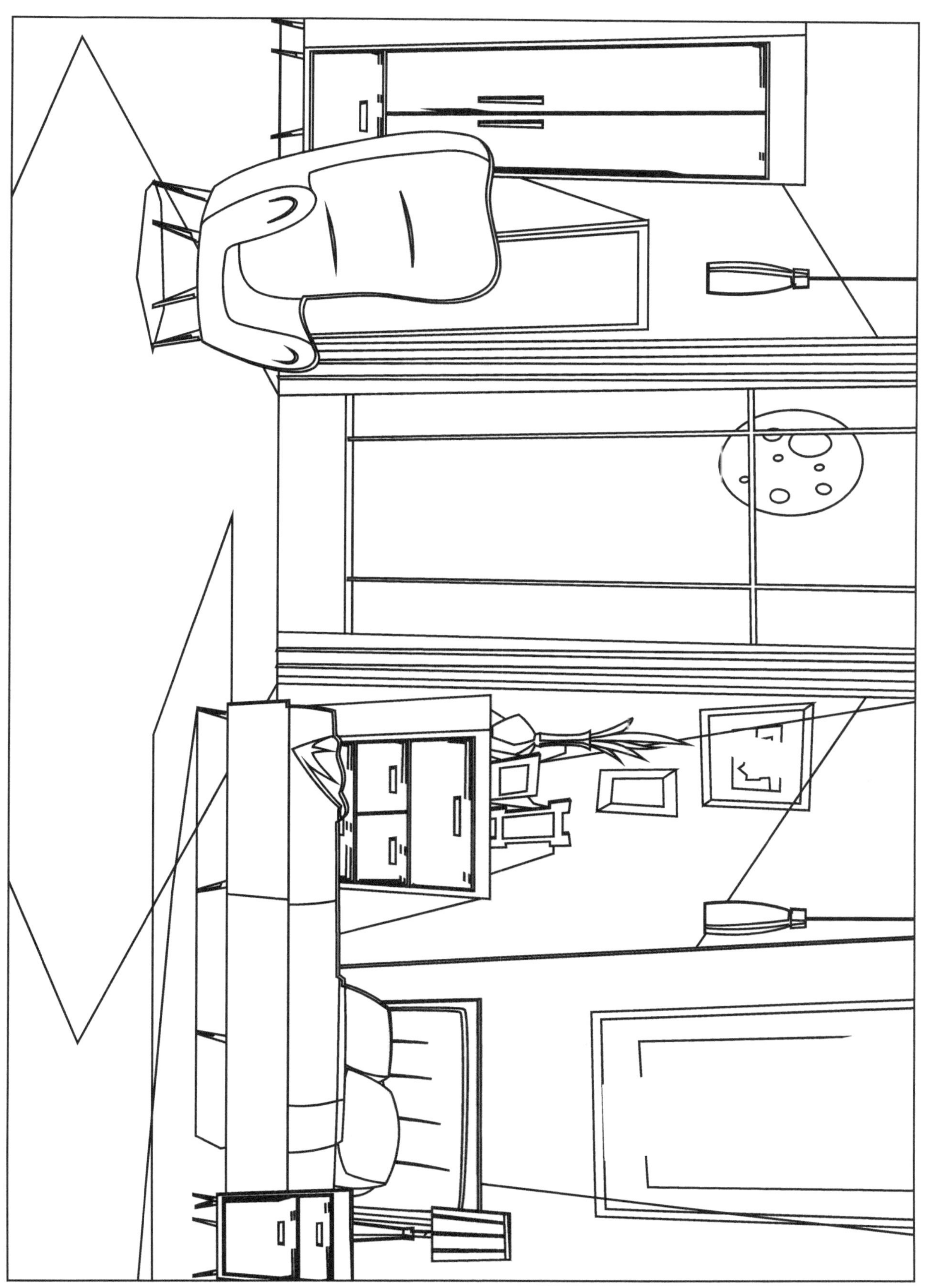

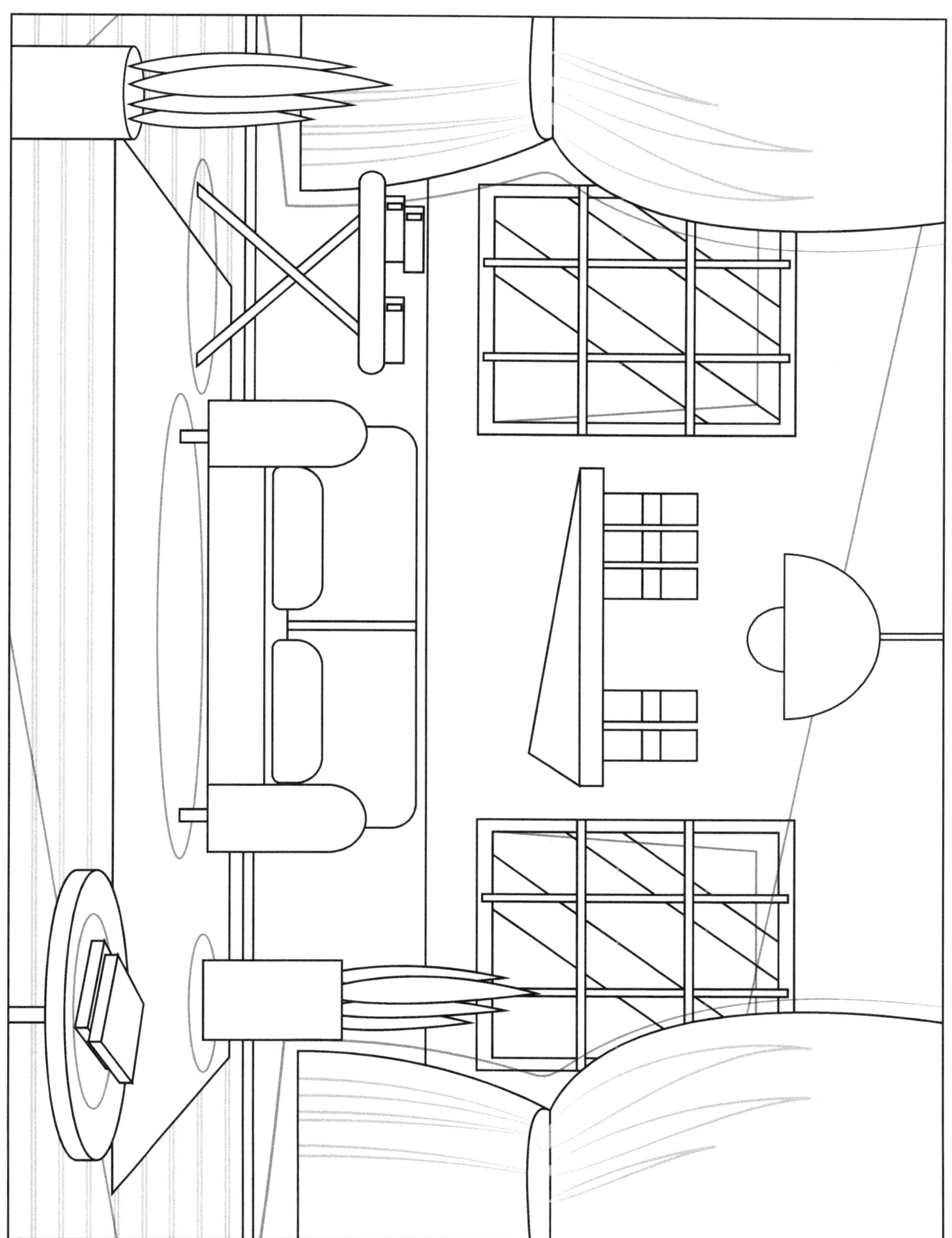

living room

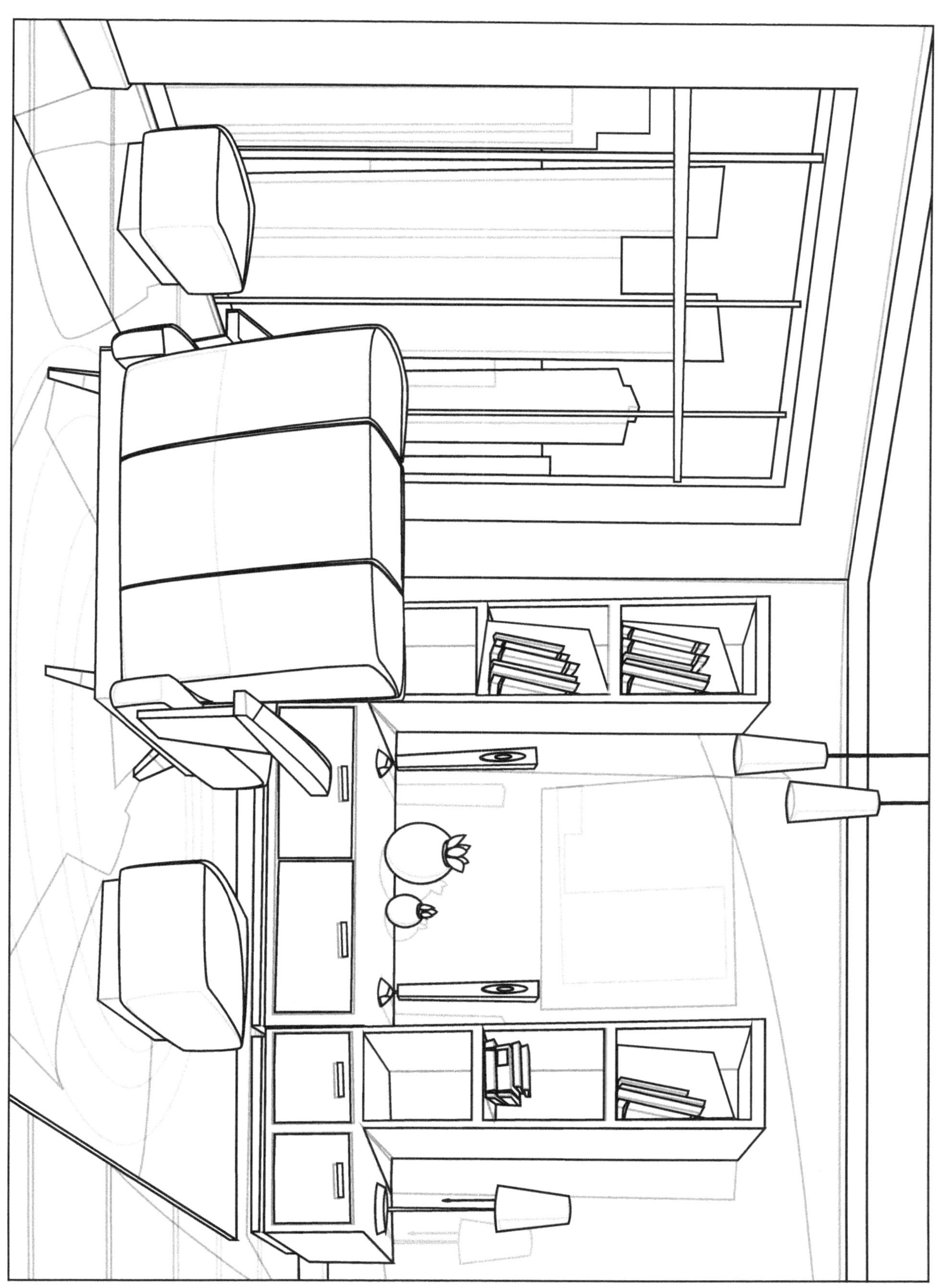

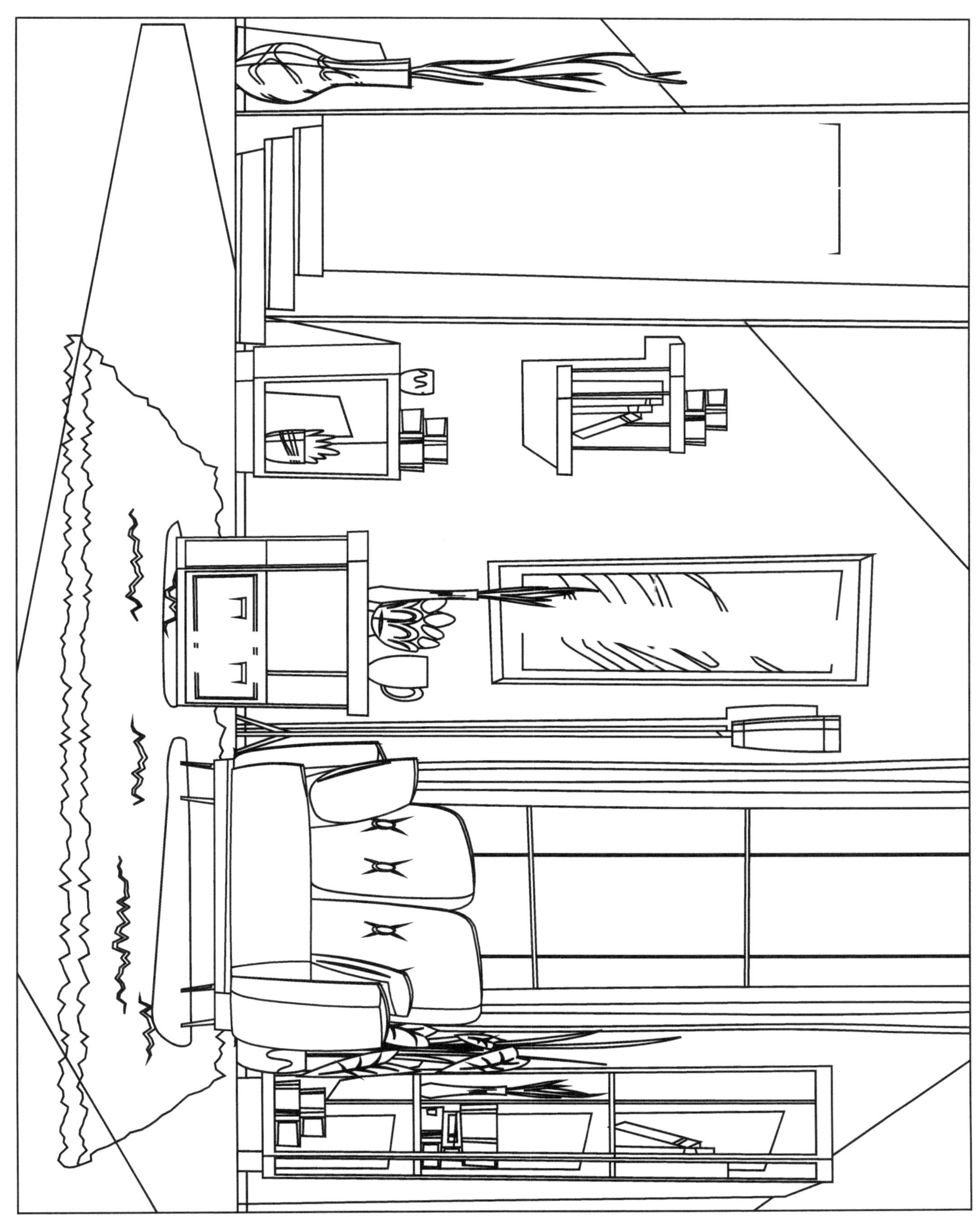

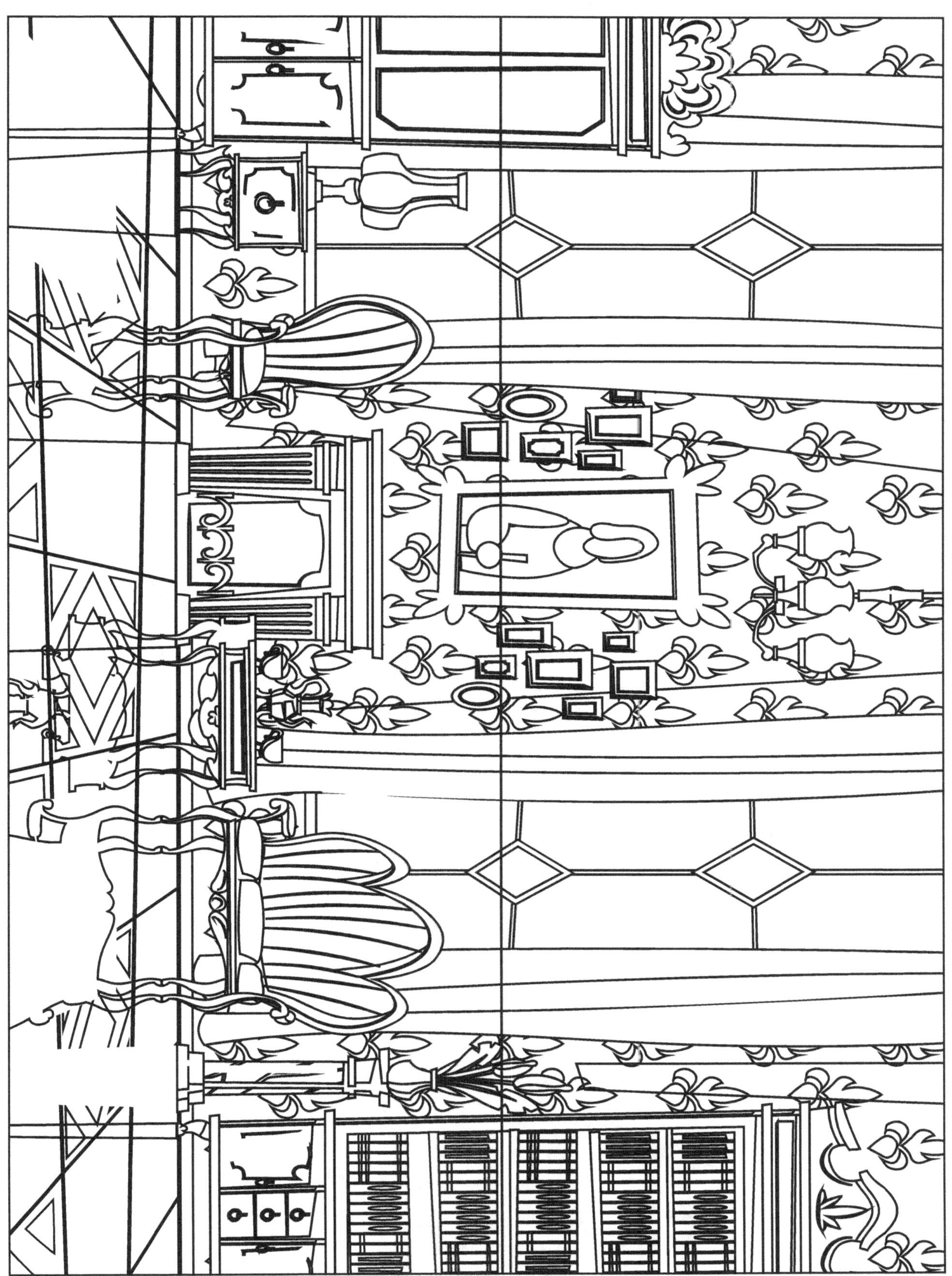

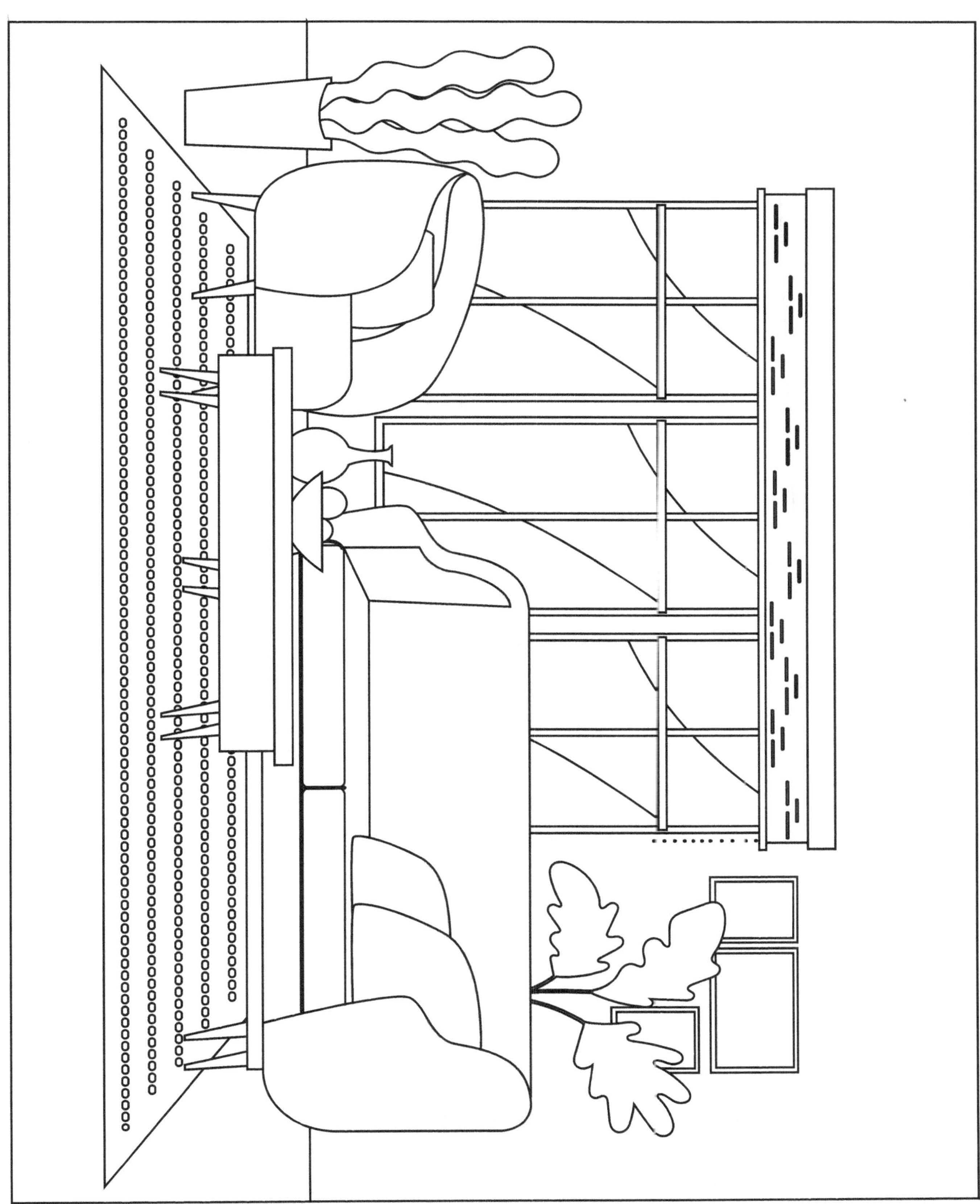

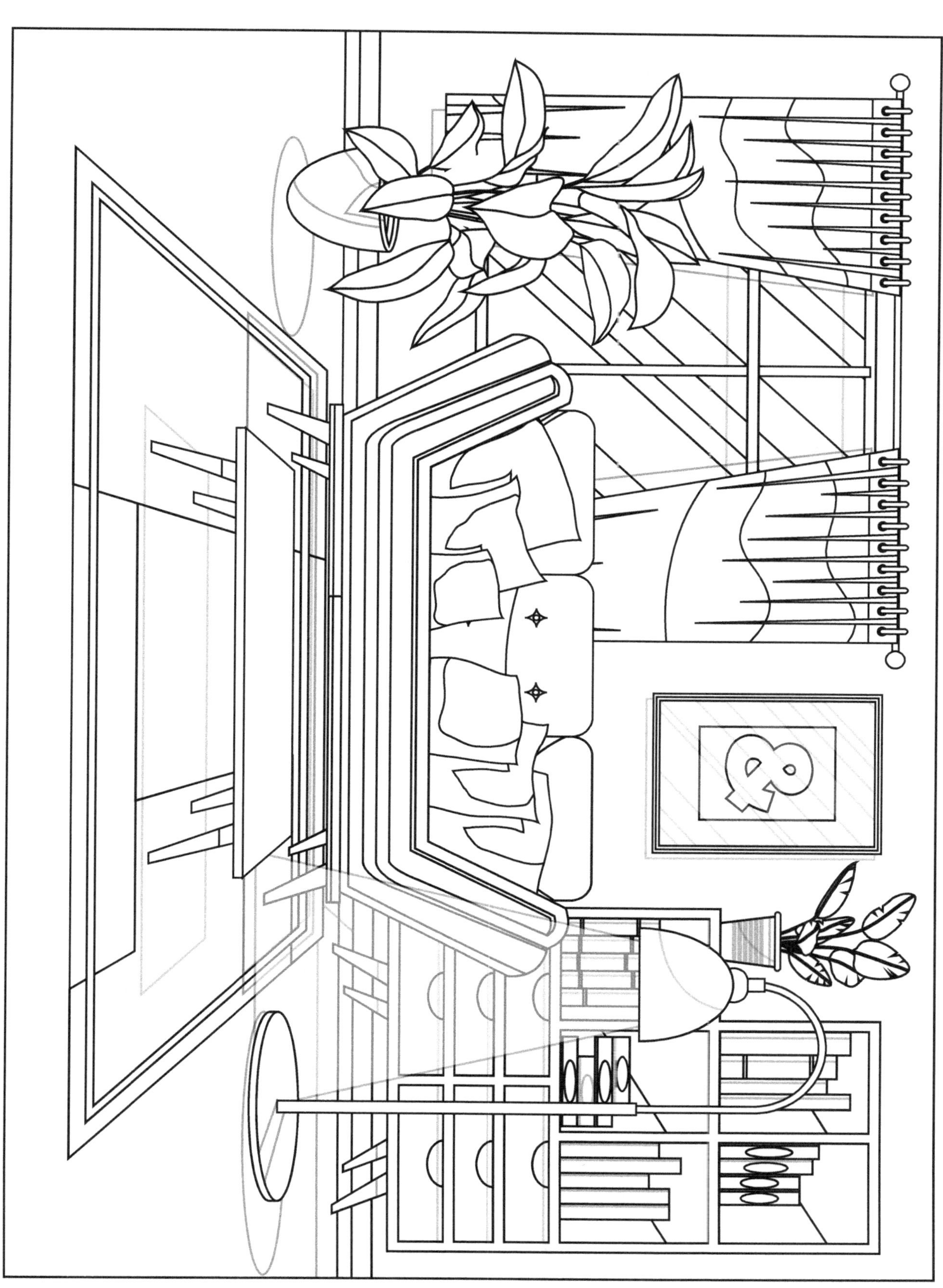

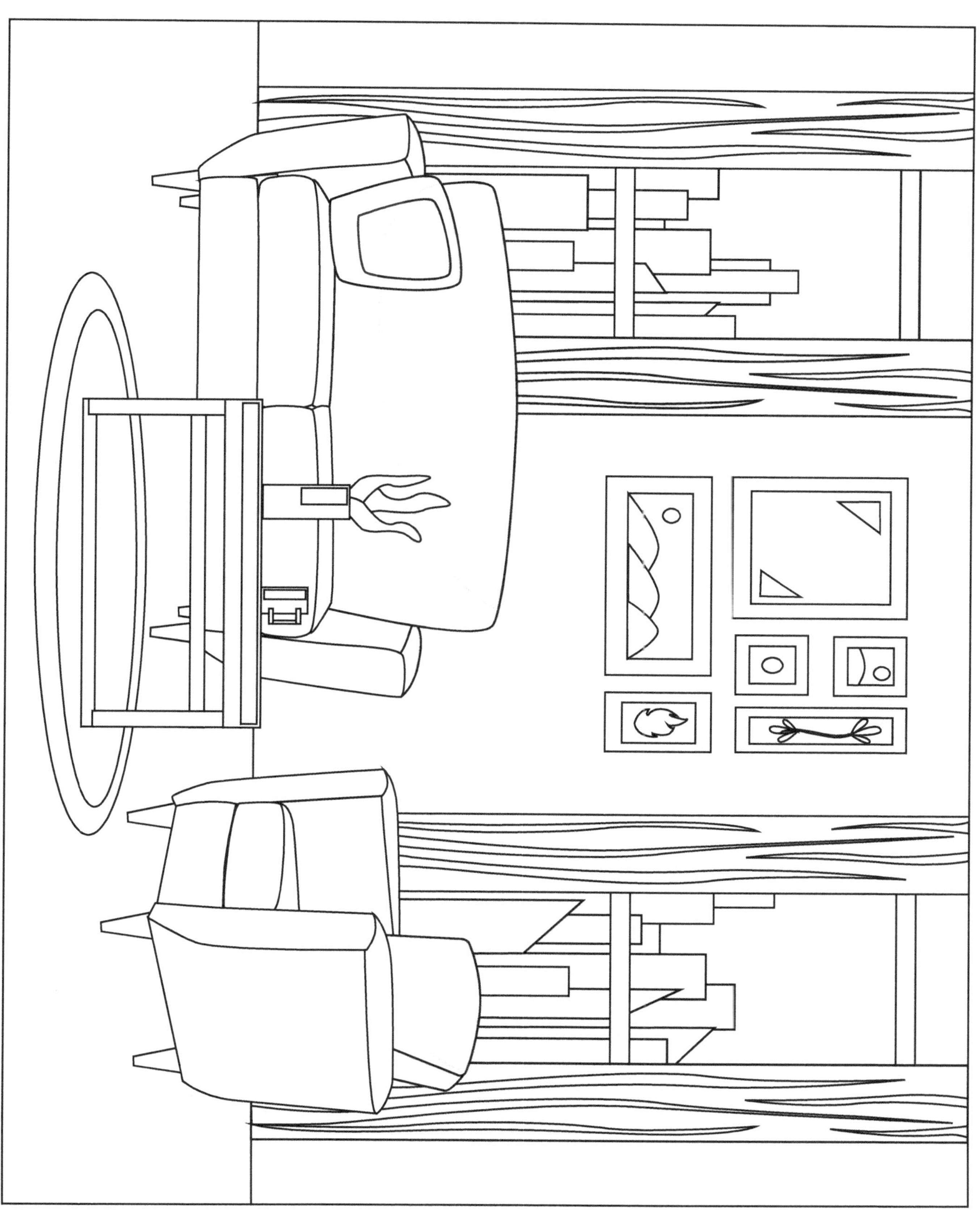

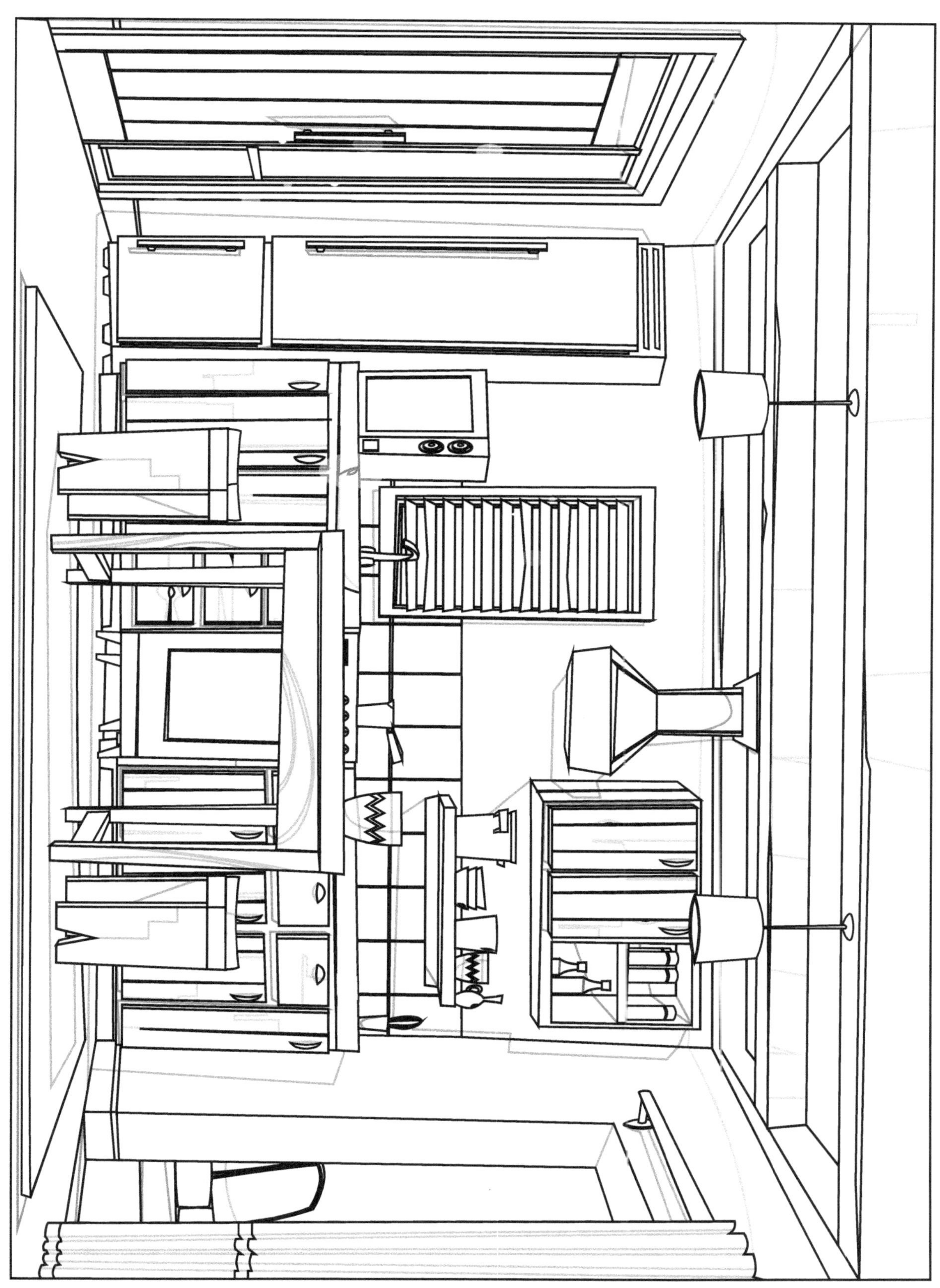